Smith

The last blue whale

THE LAST BLUE WHALE

THE LAST
BLUE WHALE

by

Vincent Smith

Illustrated by Wilson Buchanan

Published in San Francisco by

Harper & Row, Publishers

New York Hagerstown San Francisco London Sydney

To Susan
And to Sascha, Jake and Daniel, that they'll
know whales

Special thanks to Joy Lee and Project Jonah Australia

THE LAST BLUE WHALE.
Copyright © 1979 by Vincent Smith
Illustrations Copyright © 1979 by Wilson Buchanan
All rights reserved. Printed in Australia. No part of this book may be used or
reproduced in any manner whatsoever without written permission except in the case
of brief quotations embodied in critical articles and reviews. For information address
Harper & Row, Publishers, Inc., 10 East 53rd Street, New York, N.Y. 10022.

Originally published by Harper & Row (Australasia) Pty. Ltd. under the title MUSCO
—BLUE WHALE

FIRST U.S. EDITION

ISBN 0–06–250920–9

LIBRARY OF CONGRESS CATALOG CARD NUMBER: 78–66387

Typeset, printed and bound by Academy Press Pty. Ltd., Brisbane, Australia.

1

Musco whaled a boom of delight, as happy Blue whales do. He could feel the water getting warmer as it brushed past his great body. His sense system commanded a drop in body temperature to compensate and told him it was good.

Musco wanted to say so.

Musco and his mother and father were cruising at a steady eight or nine knots north from the Antarctic into warmer waters. The feeding season was over and they were in the peak of physical condition, their blubber rich enough in oil to last the fasting season in the tropics, till they returned again to graze on the Antarctic summer crop of krill, the little shrimps that swarmed each year in the cold, swirling water.

Musco's mother was ready to calve the infant which had been conceived eleven months ago in the same warm water where it would be born. But she felt no need to hurry. They'd reach the place in ample time if they kept up this steady pace, even though they'd lingered in the south till the last of the krill had disappeared and the plankton on which the little shrimps fed had been killed off by the darkening sky as the winter closed in.

Away to the east of the three whales were the jagged limestone and endless glaring white sand dunes of the West Australian coast, harbouring pockets of people in tiny, isolated towns.

Musco gave the people a fleeting thought.

He had never seen people. And though he knew whales were in the oceans years before people appeared on the land, he couldn't quite comprehend how anything survived on that barren, forbidding land to the east. There gusting winds often hurled themselves out across the water, searing the lungs and backs of cruising whales as they humped and dived.

He knew that people had come in ships which killed and had slaughtered whales in their thousands. Beautiful, gentle whales had died in the most horrible way, and had been made to float and to bob upturned on the surface after death instead of being allowed to slip into the private dignity of the sea.

The ships still came and whales still died but, perplexingly, families like Musco's, Blue whale families, were seldom attacked.

As Blue whales mostly do, Musco's family was keeping well away from land, keeping the clear blue Indian Ocean deeps beneath them. They were much bigger than other sorts of whale and felt awkward and cramped when the water was shallow. It made them feel ill at ease when they were in range of the people on land.

Today they told each other how good they felt in bursts of song.

Because he felt happy Musco put on a burst of speed, accelerated to about twenty knots, his tail flukes undulating so that they sent a charge of excitement through his whole being. He was exhilarated by the sheer comprehension of the power he could develop. He slowed and surfaced to blow, sending a plume of air and fine spray thirty feet into the air. Three big gulps of air, a fourth, and down. He dived deep, a hundred feet or more before turning and pushing as he had never pushed the water before. Rushing upwards bringing every muscle into play, all the power he could find . . . this was being alive. The crystal sparkle of the surface came nearer and with one final, massive effort, Musco hurled himself into the air.

Everything stopped. For a split second, that infinitely small moment between up and down, Musco's massive body tightened and

BLUE WHALE

he experienced an orgasmic crescendo of emotion and sensation, of what it was to be a whale—big, powerful, gentle, graceful, loving and loved—at peace with the world, the sky, the ocean and all its creatures.

He relaxed and crashed to the surface in a volcano of white water.

Musco righted himself and headed slowly to the surface for a long blow. This was what it was to be a Blue whale. And he loved it.

At thirteen years Musco was beginning to feel his krill, like the known and unknown brothers and sisters before him. He had tried to articulate whale puberty to his parents, but the combination of sounds wouldn't come. They conceived, though, through thought and through instinct, what he was trying to communicate. They sensed it and he sensed it.

Together the three understood that on this voyage north Musco would leave the family group, perhaps forever, perhaps not, to try to find a female . . . a mate to make love to, to love, to create another whale life . . . a mate to spend a lifetime with. Sexual maturity had touched Musco deeply and it would develop in the coming months. But he was far from physically mature. It wasn't likely he would reach physical maturity for at least another five or six seasons, growing all the time.

Even now, for a pubescent Blue whale, he was big. At full size he promised to be a giant among giants. He was already over eighty feet long. Blue whales, Musco knew, were the biggest of all the whales, which made them the biggest creatures ever to inhabit the earth.

The trio had slowed now and were moving at a casual three or four knots. Arching up through the water to blow, Musco looked like a neckless dinosaur—only bigger. The satin skin of mottled blue-grey encased a surprisingly slim body that tapered like a torpedo to the horizontal tail flukes which gave him power—the flukes that smacked into the water as he sounded and which he loved to crash down onto the surface while doing a sort of whale head-stand. Mostly he'd do it for his own amusement. Sometimes for the amusement of others.

To a human, Musco would have looked as though he had a permanent smile. His cavernous mouth almost closed, curved upwards and back to a point well back along his body, just below what seemed a pinpoint eye, a clear eye but one which saw little but worked more as part of a team of senses. Some feet back from his eyes, but almost in line with them, Musco used a pair of fins to help in a small way with the swimming—indeed, if Musco or any other Blue whale stopped swimming they would drown.

He could almost float without swimming but not quite. Much of a Blue whale—more than half the blubber, about a third of the oil-filled bones and a little of the flesh—is lighter than sea water; his blood is less salty than the sea and is thus lighter; and his lungs are evenly spread beneath his backbone which allows more bouyancy. Even with this help Musco's tail and fins were in perpetual motion. He would find during this season in the tropics that his fins had other uses. He would learn what it meant to caress, rather than be caressed.

Beneath what was a quite rugged chinline, the mottled grey–blue lightened to a softer colour which ranged from musty sulphur near his mouth to cream on the forebelly, where the long, concertina grooves ended and his skin smoothed out again. The grooves stretched from his chin back about half the length of the body. Now they were tightly held together, but they would distend so that his whole belly became a smooth balloon while he fed, sieving krill from the water with the feathery baleen that hung into his mouth like a curtain from his upper gums.

The fine misty spout from Musco's blow-hole shot into the air and was snuffed out, gone, before the whale took another breath.

Above the whales the air was still. They were now well north of the Southern Ocean winds. The Indian Ocean was calmer than the Southern, its water glassy at times, and today the air didn't seem to care whether Musco's spouts went one way or another, if they went anywhere. The young whale cared where he was going and now he was about 100 miles west of that vast stretch of West Australian coast.

In the water everything Musco felt, everything he sensed, was good. There was a twinge of misgiving at the thought of leaving his parents. But it soon went. For the Blue whale is a family whale. And he wanted to build a family. Musco wanted a family for his own very private reasons, to satisfy a heartfelt urge.

But there was also a more pragmatic impulse, a need to perpetuate the species. He was well aware that the population of Blue whales had dwindled in recent times—from around two hundred thousand who made their summer homes in the Antarctic and a few thousand in other oceans, down to perhaps five thousand altogether. It was only when men realised the Blue whale was at the edge of obliteration that the killer ships stopped coming. Meanwhile more than sixty thousand had been snatched from the sea in twenty-five seasons.

It was no vain or proud impulse in Musco. It was his realisation that Blue whales were as one with the ocean and therefore the ocean would suffer if they no longer existed, that swelled his need to have a family.

It was a knowledge, at one level of his mind a misty sort of understanding, at another quite sharply defined, that there was reason for the differences between Blue whales and other members of the whale order. Musco had always recognised that as well as Blues there were many other different whales. He'd been aware of their presence, mostly through encounters during the summer feeding season in the Antarctic, but he'd also accumulated knowledge from his parents in far greater detail than that provided by mere experience.

It was this picture of a big, complicated life-pattern in whales that impressed Musco as a special one within the vast and truly awesome matrix of the ocean itself. He was a part of it all.

As he swam Musco summoned the pattern into his consciousness from the depths of his learning. It was vivid.

Not unnaturally, he saw Blue whales at the centre of the scheme —for in his mind all other whales, all other creatures, related to the Blue whale. He saw the things that made Blues so different from others, apart from their enormous size: their almost exclusive diet of krill, their habit of feeding only during the summer when the krill massed in the Antarctic, their irregular migrations northward to winter in Equatorial waters and their preference for the open ocean rather than coastal waters.

And yet there were similarities that made Blues—along with Humpback, Minke, Sei, Bryde's, and Fin whales—one family, that of the rorqual whales. They all had grooved throats and a dorsal fin. But even within that family there was a special sub-family grouping for the Humpbacks because of the things that set them apart from their closest relatives.

Musco had seen many Humpbacks. He had seen them more in his infancy, ten seasons ago, than he did now, and often in this part of the ocean. But he didn't see them much any more. He admired the way they sang—their especially beautiful, mournful sounds which echoed through the oceans, sometimes from hundreds of miles away, for up to four hours at a time.

He liked Humpbacks. They were definitely members of the rorqual family. But they had black backs instead of the blue grey of the others. And they weren't nearly as streamlined or handsome. They had nobbly, lumpy heads and usually had barnacles growing on their skin, because they swam so slowly. Apart from their song what endeared them to Musco physically was their flippers, by far the biggest on any whale and scalloped irregularly along the leading edge. It wasn't so much the look of them that Musco liked, but the way they were used; he'd seen Humpbacks almost locked in embrace and he'd seen a mother Humpback cuddle her calf.

Once Musco had played with a group of Humpback youngsters. They were especially athletic and were able to leap clear of the water much more easily than Musco with his great bulk. The biggest Humpback grew not much more than about forty feet. But Musco's massive strength and streamlined body more than matched the agility of the stocky Humpbacks.

Musco much preferred his own tightly knit family unit but he admired the cooperation of the much larger Humpback groups where the babies actually had aunts as well as their mothers to care for them.

Humpbacks were especially fine whales. But even though they loved to play Musco noticed a nervousness about them. He speculated this was so because they could not fully believe that killer ships would no longer chase them, as they no longer chased Blues.

But not so the Fin whales, perhaps the nearest relative of the Blues. They were almost as big and similar in appearance, except for the odd colouring of their lower jaws which were blueish grey to the left and white to the right. The Fins never came quite as far into the ice as the Blues did during the summer, and in winter they headed north like the Blues but never went as far as the warm tropical waters in which Musco and his family spent their winters. Musco felt sorry for the Fins because they were easy prey for the killer ships without the protection of the ice. And like the Humpback, there were now fewer of them, too.

He felt sorry, also, for the tiny Minke whales which grew to only about thirty feet and were the smallest of the rorquals. As the Fins had become harder to find, they too were chased a lot by the killer ships, particularly in the last few seasons. And they were so handsome, Musco thought, with their stark white slashes across their flippers and their creamy white baleens. Unlike the Blues they shunned tropical waters but they did swim far in the more temperate water and Musco knew he could usually see a Minke in almost any ocean of the world.

Musco had a special admiration for his cousins the Sei whales. It was they who had taught him a feeding trick that was uncommon to the Blues but which Musco liked a lot when he had seen how it was done and had mastered it: it was the method of feeding by skimming.

Most of the whales that sieve their food through baleen plates feed by gulping water and forcing it out of their mouths with their tongues, trapping the food in the baleen feathers or bristles. But Sei whales also skim along the surface with their mouths open, passing a constant stream of water through their baleens and trapping their food that way. It fascinated Musco and he practised and practised until he could do it almost as well as a Sei itself and almost as well as he could gulp. But the Sei had a much more varied diet than Musco; they ate swarming fish and little squids as well as krill and zooplankton. And this caused them to wander in fairly erratic ways in their seasonal migrations away from the cold water: they hardly ever went into the ice of the Antarctic and in the north were rarely found closer to the Pole than the Aleutian Islands. They were bigger than the Minkes and they also had been chased by the killers when the Fins became harder to find.

Musco had encountered a Bryde's whale only once, it was so rare. It looked very much like a Sei but had much shorter throat grooves, a smaller dorsal fin and its baleen was stiffer and shorter; it fed mostly on schooling fish. The encounter with the Bryde's had taken place several winters ago; these whales spent all their time in the warmer tropical and sub-tropical oceans.

All these were the whales Musco identified with most strongly; they were his closest relatives. Beyond them the pattern in Musco's mind broadened.

Next closest were the family of Right whales, big—about forty to sixty feet long—thick set and sluggish. They were so sluggish in fact, that they had been given their name many seasons back by men who came to chase whales in rowing boats and found them so easy to kill they had become the "right" whale to seek out. They were thought of differently from the rorqual whales because they had no grooves in their throats and no dorsal fins, and their baleen were long, sometimes up to fourteen feet, thin, very flexible and densely feathered.

Musco had never met the lumbering Bowhead or the Greenland Right whale, whose head made up one third of its body length. Nevertheless, his mind, drawing on thirteen years of sensory input and on its highly developed ability to perceive and visualise from information received from his parents and other whales many hundreds of miles distant, gave him a sharp and accurate picture. He could visualize quite well the great Bowhead, its mouth partly out of the water, skimming peacefully through a patch of zooplankton, its long whisps of baleen wafting in the gentle eddies of its wake.

Musco knew that the main reason he had not encountered a Bowhead was that it stayed almost strictly with the seasonal advance and retreat of the Arctic ice. He also knew that this was one whale that was once plentiful but was now on the verge of extinction, and yet still hunted by small groups of people in open boats, Eskimos. He did not know that men had considered the Bowhead exterminated until 1932, when four had been seen.

Musco worried for the lives of the Bowheads.

And he worried for their close relative, the Black Right whale, similar to the Bowhead but smaller, with a distinct map-like colour pattern on its belly and a double, vee-shaped, forward-sloping blow-hole capped with a horny sort of hat. The Black Right whales lived in three separate locations; the North Atlantic, the North Pacific and the southern Arctic. There was one further member of the Right whale family, the Pygmy Right. Musco knew of it but had never come across one.

As he'd copied from the Seis, Musco had learned another feeding trick from the Grey whales. This was to nuzzle the ocean bottom during occasional forays into shallow water, stirring up molluscs and crabs and gulping them. It was frowned upon by other Blues but Musco found it entertaining. The Greys regarded it as their special style and Musco thanked them for providing him with the opportunity to share it when he fed this way. It was a method of feeding that led the Greys to be different from the other baleen whales, to become a separate family. Since they neither gulped nor skimmed the Greys did not need grooved throats to the same extent as their relatives, and they had only two to four short grooves. Nor had they many baleens and the fringes on these were few and far between. They had no dorsal fin but rather a dorsal hump.

The Greys were the third family group of baleen whales and with the others—the Rorquals and the Rights—made up those known to man as the Mysteceti, or moustached whales, so called by the Greeks because of the trailing feathery baleen in their mouths, a type of mucous membrane often wrongly called whalebone. All other whales, different from Musco, and very much more numerous, made up the group known to man as Odontoceti, or toothed whales.

If Musco ever felt tempted to be discouraged during difficult swims on the long migration—and these were rare, usually occurring only when he'd rather stop to play on a chance meeting with Humpbacks—he thought of the Grey whales. The Greys made the longest migration of any known mammal, sometimes up to sixteen thousand miles in a season. They clung close to the coasts and Musco did not approve of their habit of entering shallow water to breed and calve. Musco thought that to be very risky, a habit which Humpbacks had wisely stopped in many places when they realised the dangers.

It had been a disastrous habit for the Greys. Many seasons ago there had been western Greys which migrated between Korea and the Sea of Okhostsk and the killer ships obliterated them. Musco mourned the loss of the western Greys: he was sure they were no more. The eastern Greys, which clung to the American Pacific coast, had been more lucky. They were no longer heavily hunted and, unlike other sorts of whales which had been savagely slaughtered before the killer ships stopped coming for them, they had been able to grow in numbers again.

Musco hoped this could happen to the Blue whales. It gave great purpose to his approaching winter in the tropics and strengthened his determination to find a mate and build a family.

2

Alan Burton sucked on the upended ten ounce glass of light bitter beer until it had disappeared down his throat. He plonked the glass on to the bar, foam drifting down the insides, and dragged a hairy, sweaty arm across his mouth. A hair caught in the two-day stubble on his chin and he grimaced slightly as hair and beard pulled against each other.

"Give us another one, love. Quick. That didn't even touch the sides."

The barmaid pulled another pot and the foam hardly had time to slip down the outside of the glass and soak into the strip of patterned towelling that ran half the length of the bar for such a purpose, before Burton took it and quaffed it. He really was dry.

Carnarvon was like that most of the time—thirsty.

The river at Carnarvon, the Gascoyne, isn't really a river at all. It's a snaking watercourse that is dry in winter, save for a few waterholes, and which floods in a torrent during the summer wet. At Carnarvon it twists its way through banana plantations, which suck their water in pipes from below its dry bed, and then it opens into a mangrove tidal flat and yawns into the sea.

To the south there is nothing for miles but flat salty plains of sand and spinifex grass until the hamlets of aptly named Shark Bay. The northern reach is much the same until a small jetty marks the US North West Cape Communications Centre, part of the world-wide Polaris submarine network. East of Carnarvon the plains rise through handsome, rugged gorges to a low plateau where Merino sheep grow beautiful wool on an acre or two each, fighting kangaroos for every blade of grass, and where iron miners rip their riches from the ground and send them to Japan at the rate of half a million dollars a day.

Carnarvon got to be where it was because of wool. Ships called there to take the fleece 500 miles south to Perth, the most isolated State capital in the world. It had become the road-head for that vast north-western quarter of Australia, and still the wool came in to be trucked south. But now the road runs farther north and except for its fruits and vegetables for the southern capital, its wool and NASA tracking station, it is mostly a town for getting through on the way north or south—a place to rest and wet the throat.

In the early 1960s Carnarvon had Babbage Island, a land-based whaling station. It had been home for three catcher ships that dragged bloated corpses of great whales back to shore for flensing and rendering into inanimate products far more prosaic, far less heroic than the life they had come from.

Alan Burton had been fascinated by Babbage Island.

He'd read *Moby Dick* once and was enthralled when he first drove his big jinkered truck into Carnarvon to drop drums of diesel oil and kerosene. He visited Babbage Island the first chance he had. It was out of season and the station wasn't operating. But he'd been allowed to look over it and as he stood on the station jetty and smelled the ocean he could see in his mind the modern Captain Ahabs bringing in their rich catch after a death defying struggle against the elements. It was easy to romanticise when he didn't see the reality.

He didn't go again but he began to read more about whaling. He'd been swept up by its romance. A man, making a living a tough way, pushing a truck, he identified with the rugged whalers as history portrayed them.

When Babbage Island was closed in 1963 because the Humpback whales came no more and the three catcher ships were up for sale, Burton thought only briefly. He figured he could make just as good a living hauling goods on a small ship as he could pushing a truck through the dust—probably better, with the chance of servicing the mining and oil exploration bases that were beginning to dot themselves along the northern coast.

The hundred feet of steel ship went for a song, much less than he got for his truck. There was enough for the refit and change that was needed to turn the ageing Gascoyne Star into a coastal trader and occasional lobster catcher.

He'd left the harpoon gun in place in the bows. It distinguished the ship somehow. And he kept its mechanism in working order out of pride for the boat as much as for the vicarious romance that it indulged him.

The Gascoyne Star hadn't made Burton rich, but it had kept him happy, and easy going. In the Pier Hotel, right at the foot of the Carnarvon town jetty, where the Star was made fast, Alan Burton belched quietly to himself. "Give us another when you're right love", he called to the barmaid.

~~~ &~~~

That afternoon, out in the Indian Ocean, Musco thought of the good things. He noticed that his father had quickened the pace a little and turned so that they were now headed north west.

Musco knew where his father was taking them. His highly developed brain had a specific memory map—a legacy from his pre-historic ancestors, the freshwater river dolphins which still survived after some forty million years. Environment had helped to develop the river dolphins' sense of echolocation, their means of navigation in the hazard ridden flooded rivers and lakes of India, South America and China. Since the water in those rivers was so muddy vision was of little use and some species, like the Ganges

MUSCO

River Dolphins even lost it altogether in favour of total echolocation, bouncing impulses off objects in the murk and building up from these impulses a complete mind-picture of the environment. Once built, that mind-picture remained stored in the brain, as a map which could be called upon in the future, and which could be built upon with information from other whales.

Today, Musco knew exactly where he was, how far away the nearest land was, how deep the ocean beneath him and the shape of its floor. And the map told him where they were going.

On this course, Musco knew, they were heading for the Chagos Archipelago where three seasons back, when his brother was still with them, they had broken the winter fast and feasted on red pelagic crabs. That season had been one long family picnic until his brother decided to leave them. Musco felt a great loss when his brother, after eleven seasons, had left the family group, as other brothers and sisters had before him, and sought a life shared with a mate.

Musco had rationalised the inevitability of that loss on the journey back to the Antarctic summer and now he comforted himself with the thought that his parents would make the same only slightly troubled transition when he left. But, of course, they'd still be three for the southward journey again anyway, after the birth of the calf.

It would be female, Musco mused as he basked on the surface blowing casually three or four times in the space of ten minutes and making a shallow dive to close the widening gap between him and his parents. He didn't know why it would be a female, he just thought it would. He'd know her, briefly, before going off alone.

They would have the calf and they would have the memories of all their other young. They would have the whale history, the story of the Blue whale going back to the time when two hundred thousand in small family groups were scattered across almost all the world's southern oceans, migrating rhythmically between the Antarctic and the tropics. And in the north, where Musco had never been there were five thousand who summered in the Pacific Arctic. Now there were about six thousand of Musco's Antarctic Blues and about fifteen hundred in the north.

Long before his father was a young whale, the ships with sails

BLUE   WHALE

had dropped smaller boats over their sides and tried to attack Blue whales with steel lances. But the whales swam too fast for the small boats with men straining at their oars.

It was the first time any other creature had tried to harm a fit Blue whale. The Bowheads and the Rights, the Greys, the Sperms had been killed by people in such boats, the whales that couldn't swim as fast as Blues and Fins.

It hadn't been until his father was a calf of a couple of seasons that the slaughter of the Blue whales began.

The ships had changed. They had motors and could move as fast as a Blue but still the puny spears couldn't stop a great whale at full speed. But in time men found a way to hunt Blues. The ships with motors came not with spears but with harpoons that would penetrate deep inside a whale before exploding and shattering the vital organs. When that weapon was used against the great Blues there was no mercy. One in every three Blue whales died in one season.

Like his father, Musco had never understood why whales were killed in that way at all. And, while he never fully understood the link, he perceived that there was a connection between the end of mass killing of one family of whales and the small numbers of those whales left in the sea.

He realised that the killer ships had stopped chasing Blues when there were so few Blues in the sea that there was a real danger they might not be able to produce calves fast enough to ensure the whole family lived on. In Musco's experience, ships were safe for Blue whales. He had heard stories of one or two Blues being killed, but this was very rare and when it had happened it had been all the more shocking for being unexpected.

Even though the mass killing had stopped before Blues were snuffed as a family from the ocean there was still a grave danger that they might not survive. The danger was even greater for the Bowheads and the other Rights, perhaps, but not so great for the Humpbacks and the Greys who were no longer hunted.

Just as he perceived but did not understand the connection between the end of mass killing and the danger of imminent demise for the whale families, Musco also perceived but did not understand the chain that began with hideous death and ended with huge ships opening cavernous mouths behind them and swallowing the corpses, belching black smoke and spewing whale blood back into a sea that was alive with the cries of whale grief.

For Musco there was an uncertain comfort in the knowledge that of the twelve families which had been viciously hunted, seven were not now pursued, though they had been brought close to obliteration and might—especially in the case of the Bowhead and other Rights —disappear from the sea.

He hoped that at least the same uncertain comfort would be brought to the Fins, the Seis, the Minkes, the Sperms (or Cachalots).

Cachalots were another family altogether and Musco's mind shaped yet another pattern for him, relating the Cachalots to Blues. He saw a picture of the much more populous Odontocenti whales, the toothed whales, of which the Cachalots were a member. The Cachalots were the biggest of the toothed whales—a big one would be almost as big as Musco now, about sixty feet long, with a great box head and a narrow, toothed jaw swung out beneath.

While Musco identified with the Cachalots in many ways he was aware of the marked differences. Cachalots did not graze but chased giant squid in the dark depths of the ocean, far deeper than most Blue whales could go without risking death from the great pressure. Nor did they choose one mate but rather kept harems, which did not diminish the respect and affection between them, but probably accounted for their great population. Even so, while their numbers were great throughout the ocean, there were many places where Cachalots were no longer encountered.

The Bowheads and other Rights had suffered most during the period when the big ships, flimsy as they were, first began to chase whales. But more recently over a quarter million Cachalots had been slaughtered by the fast motor ships with their ghastly weapons— more than any other family.

The number of Cachalots in the sea—originally, perhaps a million —did not diminish that horror for Musco.

He felt empathy there. And he felt it as he did with the countless other toothed whale families, the many different dolphins, the porpoises, the beaked whales, the white whales, and the river dolphins. He felt it because for all their physical differences they were indeed one great family.

He pondered the differences, some of them spectacular, like the two teeth of the Narwhal which corkscrewed out from the fifteen foot body to become a spear-like tusk of eight or ten feet, making it look like an aquatic unicorn.

Musco also recalled the Ganges River Dolphin which was the father of echolocation, perhaps the most important of Musco's abilities, and the Chinese Lake Dolphin, known to live only in the Yangtse River and Tung ting Hu Lake, never venturing towards the open sea but, like a salmon, travelling many miles upriver into tiny tributaries to breed.

Musco also knew the elegant, pure white Beluga whale, the chatterbox of the sea, which travels in groups of hundreds but which dies in thousands, in an uncontrolled slaughter at the hands of killer ships, like many other of the small toothed whales, to provide food for minks.

He found it hard to love the Orca but he did, from afar, for Musco knew of the packs of killer whales which sometimes hunted down a wounded baleen whale, or one that was aged and suffering arthritis or a weak heart. He respected them because they killed for food. The killer ships were inanimate and did not need food and the people on them could not possibly have appetites that demanded such monstrous carnage.

In his mind Musco was able to visualise some sixty-seven different families of toothed whales, clearly ranged in an order that distinguished one from the other by physical appearance, by habit and behaviour.

That was wondrous enough in itself to Musco. But even more wondrous was the fact that he could visualise such a thing, that he could know it so clearly.

His knowledge of the ocean, of the vast whale family, often left Musco breathless. And then he would realise that he even understood how and why he knew, and that was sometimes awesome for him.

3

It was on routine days such as this one that Musco had shared with his father, his mother, other whales, the communication, the encyclopaedic bursts of information that were conscious and direct and which could be transferred from whale to whale sometimes at speeds up to half a million signals of knowledge in half an hour. And with it the much more ethereal absorption and exchange, the gestalt, that built Musco's knowledge.

There had been many such days for Musco—days when he and his father might exchange the sum total of their knowledge, unconsciously review it, and in doing so increase it.

There had been many such days for Blue whales before him so that with each generation the mass of knowledge of the ocean and of themselves, gained through experience, perception of their environment and perception of themselves, exploded.

Now, at puberty, Musco could plumb his origins and the forty million years of change and growth from whale to whale since the

BLUE WHALE

archeocetaceans forsook their landbound mammal brothers and mysteriously returned to the water from which all life sprang. He could see the physical development that took place with each new whale, and specifically with each new Blue whale; the subtle, slow, inexorable changes over a time span that Musco's mind could deal with momentarily. They were physical changes that were determined by the watery environment, by its demands which were so different from the atmospheric environment of people.

Land limbs transformed to swimming limbs, flippers and tail flukes, and since the water's buoyancy opposed gravity so well muscles were now used to propel the massive body through the water. Vision adapted to the diminished light below the surface.

As land-bound mammals Musco's ancient ancestors could control their body heat by sweating, but in the salty ocean they changed, for they couldn't drink to replace lost moisture. Their heads became bigger and more important in sense transmission and reception than the rest of their bodies, dominating their bodies physically and allowing the capacity for more subtle internal developments—for these reasons Musco was able to know the things he knew.

Over many generations, the whale's ability to hear and communicate had responded to the fact that sound travels three times faster in water than it does in air. In Musco's watery world sound dominated the senses: the images in his mind were acoustic rather than visual, but as real and complete as the images in any human mind.

Today, as he swam in the warm Indian Ocean, Musco did not have to tell his father how beautiful he felt. It emanated from his body and his father knew it—echolocation told him.

The three dimensional nature of this marvellous means of communication meant that whales knew not only the skin surface, the outward appearance of their fellows, but also the internal workings, for echoes penetrate the skin. And in finding out if his father was well today, Musco's echolocation impulsed off the skin, sent back strong signals from air-filled spaces inside his father's body like his lungs, and also from his oil-filled bones; and it explored the movement of blood as it coursed loudly through the older whale. A flutter in his father's heart movement would have been as obvious to Musco as a ripped tail fluke. All of those physiological signals Musco gleaned from an echolocation exploration of his father's well being, gave him a much wider picture as well, for these signals gave to Musco the keys to the emotions his father felt. Right now there was not a ripple of extraordinary physical function and Musco knew that all was well with his father. He, like Musco, was at peace as they ploughed through the water at a steady fifteen knots.

Musco gave his body and his mind over to enjoying that sensation. He could keep up that speed for at least another hour before resting. He felt he could keep it up forever but he sensed beginnings of tiredness in his mother and knew they would rest soon.

"Sven Foynd," said Alan Burton authoritatively. He often affected an air of cocky superiority, when he'd had half a dozen or more beers. Now he was well into his seventh and had the taste for it.

"In 1888 he made it. Revolutionised the business. Bet he made a packet . . . " "Norwegian," he added as an emphatic afterthought about the man who brought whaling's first revolution with the invention of the explosive harpoon. It was that invention, coupled with the development of steam powered whaling boats that fired their harpoons from cannons, that accelerated the taking of whales and allowed the whalers to venture much more expansively into the Antarctic in quest of the swifter whales, the Blues, Fins, Seis and Bryde's. The second revolution came in 1925 when factory ships, the mothers of fleets of killer boats, made it possible to hound whales through the oceans of the world, unleashing uncontrolled slaughter.

When it came to explosive harpoons Burton was an authority. He hadn't fired one professionally but while the Gascoyne Star looked the worse for wear, patched as needed, the harpoon gun stood out on the bow in immaculate condition, a shining figurehead that looked totally out of place on the ship. Burton never intended to use it, but keeping it in fine working trim was a spare time occupation.

"That thing of yours would have to be the last working gun in Australia outside Point Ceta."

BLUE WHALE

Dave Harris was referring to the sole operating whaling operation, near Albany, 200 miles south west of Perth where Cachalots were taken from March to December in a small patch out in the Southern Ocean.

"A museum would give its right arm to have it."

Burton agreed. "But there's no way. I've put too much time into it. And anyway she looks good where she is."

Harris had been born and schooled in Carnarvon and worked up and down the West Australian coast most of his 40 years. For the last couple he had settled for being deckhand, greaser and general rousabout aboard the Gascoyne Star. It was hardly top pay. But it was a reasonable living and a comfortable life, for the time being.

Harris had joined Burton in the pub after buying provisions. He was a dreamer who was spellbound by stories of the West Australian coast—a graveyard of Dutch trading ships from as early as the 17th century. Some of them were supposed to have carried fortunes in gold and Harris always held out the idea that one day, simply because he was there, he'd bump into one of those fortunes. He had no idea how. He just expected that one day riches would be his. He had no grand plans, just vague dreams.

The beer was beginning to have its effect as the afternoon wore on and the sun reddened, throwing its full force under the corrugated iron roof of the hotel verandah and on to the shabbily painted walls.

"You know," Harris said, "we could make our fortune with that gun."

"Yeah," said Burton without a trace of interest.

But Harris was having one of his bright ideas and he spoke rapidly. "Now listen. The Babbage station. It's still got all the works. They just shut it down and walked off." He was telling Burton nothing new.

"It wouldn't take much to get it going again. We could get a few blokes to give us a hand flensing. And I reckon we could rustle up enough forty gallon drums. There's 50 collecting rust out the back of this pub. We fill 'em up with the oil, load 'em on the Star and flog 'em to Point Ceta or someone in Fremantle. We could even take 'em to Japan ourselves. The Japs'd buy the stuff."

"All we've got to do," said Burton, slowly and sarcastically, "is find a couple of monstrous bloody whales, kill them, haul them back here, chop 'em and boil 'em down before they rot. You're bloody mad."

"I'm not," said Harris. He bought two more beers and leaned sideways on the bar, thrusting his face earnestly at Burton. He was settling in to make his idea sound workable.

By eight o'clock, with a mediocre Chinese meal from the sleazey café alongside the pub resting heavily in his stomach, already awash with beer, Burton was beginning to think that he'd hit Harris if he didn't shut up.

Harris had roped in Charlie Fraser who lived in as caretaker at the abandoned whaling station and made a living doing odd jobs. He was utterly, drunkenly confident that within two weeks he could have Babbage Island back in working order. "They just closed it down in '63 and I've kept her spic and span since then," he insisted, and despite the circumstances he spoke the truth. He was equally confident about rustling up two thousand forty-gallon drums for the oil.

Fraser reckoned all they had to do was steam out of Carnarvon, directly west, and lie in wait for the Blue whales he knew migrated at that time to their breeding grounds in the north. If they were patient, they'd find some.

"Two big ones'll do the trick," he declared.

Burton didn't believe he was serious.

When he woke next day in the cramped cabin-cum-wheelhouse of the Gascoyne Star Burton felt very dry in the mouth and not very healthy. Harris, standing over him, had brought hot black coffee from the galley below. He looked dreadful, too.

Burton shunned the coffee and bumped his way across the wheelhouse to the small gas refrigerator and grabbed a can of beer, which he gulped thirstily. "That's better, now I'll take the coffee. Thanks, mate."

Harris, sober but suffering from a hangover, was obviously serious about his ideas of the previous night. He'd collapsed on to the bunk in his cabin almost directly below Burton's about midnight and now, at eight in the sweltering morning, he still wanted to talk about it.

Burton had expected him to forget it . . . it was just another one of those impossible schemes. But when Fraser drove his battered half ton truck out along the jetty and pulled up alongside Gascoyne

BLUE WHALE

Star, Burton knew neither he nor Harris planned to forget it. In the tray of Fraser's truck was a six horsepower air compressor and a hundred feet of one-inch plastic hose.

"You'll need this stuff," he called up to Harris as he climbed aboard.

Fraser was more enthusiastic than he had been last night. "I got up early this morning." Fifty years of practice at beer drinking had given Fraser a pudding belly and amazing recuperative powers. "I've been doing some sums," he said.

Fraser had been doing his homework, using reference books which he'd used for his spiel to visitors when Babbage Island was still open for public inspection, though it had not processed a whale for more than fifteen years. As part of the job of resident caretaker it was his duty—he saw it as such—to guide curious visitors through the ghost-station.

"They reckon," said Fraser, "that a good whale—that'd be say a Blue, a decent sized whale—will give you about 350 barrels of oil. A barrel's thirty-one-and-a-half gallons.

"But let's look at it conservatively. OK? I rang a mate of mine in Perth this morning. Used to be in the whaling game. Industrial chemicals now. Sells the stuff they produce from Point Ceta. Works for a company called Delta Chemicals. Now they do the stuff up in five gallon lots and wholesale it at around thirty three bucks a throw. Well let's figure a barrel at thirty gallons. That's a hundred and ninety eight bucks wholesale, a barrel. Call it two hundred, right?"

Burton nodded. Harris was listening intently.

"Now, let's suppose we get a decent sized Blue. We ought to get about 350 barrels out of that, as I said before. Just figure it out. I did it on a bit of paper this morning. Comes out to seventy thousand dollars. Two the same size and we get a hundred and forty."

Burton was showing intense interest now, though he suspected the accuracy of Fraser's arithmetic. Harris's jaw dropped.

Fraser continued. "That's over forty five grand each."

Harris was slapping his knee and laughing and staring wide-eyed at Burton, who was just grinning.

"You make it sound too good to be true, Charlie," said Burton cautiously.

"Gospel, mate," said Fraser, placing a hand over his heart. "That *is* probably pitching it a bit high. Like I said, let's be conservative. Say we get one whale or a couple of small ones. Then we've got half the oil I think we can get. And say we sell it at half the wholesale price—our costs and a discount for cash and so on. That's still over twenty grand each. I don't see any way we can make less than twenty grand. For two weeks work."

He stared at Burton who was leaning backwards against the Gascoyne Star's wheel and sucking on another can of beer.

"You've got me," said Harris. "You, Al?"

"Reckon we might be in it," said Burton. "Now this mate of yours in Perth, Charlie. Is he a buyer?"

"No risk, mate. Says he'll take as much as we can give him," said Fraser.

"That's no problem," said Harris.

Fraser went on. He had indeed done his homework thought Burton. "I'll drop dead if I can't get at least three hundred forty-gallon drums, more if we need them, in good nick, with bungs fitted, lined up in a neat pile at the station inside the next two weeks. All we have to do is fill them up, ship them out on the Star from the station jetty, and pick up the cash."

"Well," said Burton. "I can't see the Star carrying three hundred full barrels of whale oil in one go. But I guess we don't have to do it all in one hit. Let's say we've found a market and we've got the transport to get the stuff to it. Can we deliver the goods? Really?"

Fraser had that covered too. "You go straight out, west, from here about two hundred, maybe three hundred miles and I'll guarantee you'll spot Blues."

"And the station, mate," said Burton, exploring all the angles. "Can we handle two big whales there?"

Fraser looked almost offended. "Now I've kept that station in working condition, more or less, almost as good as she was when they closed her down in '63. Give me two weeks and I'll have her in perfect shape to handle two big ones."

Fraser had taken literally the "care and maintenance" status the Babbage Island company had bestowed on the station when they closed it. Nobody had wanted to buy. The company, diversifying into other activities, had considered that one day it might become a worthwhile tourist attraction and might even, as a remote possibility, become a foundation on which to build a future fishery in better times.

"Don't worry about a thing at the station, mate," said Fraser. He was supremely confident.

"You really reckon you can do it?" Burton asked Fraser slowly.

"Of course he can," said Harris.

Fraser nodded. He could see the possibility of a quick killing but there was more to it. He wanted to see *his* whaling station in operation again. It would prove to him that his maintenance over the last fifteen years had been worthwhile . . . that the station could live again, if only briefly. If it could process two Blue whales under these conditions and show a profit, he'd have an argument to put to the company to consider re-opening it on a permanent basis. Fraser couldn't see the company making any other decision when confronted with such evidence.

"Pile in the truck and I'll take you out there," said Fraser. "I'll *show* you it'll work."

Fraser had been a seasonal deckhand at Babbage Island when the station opened. He'd enjoyed his work and, when the station closed in 1963 after hunting down 68 Humpbacks from an International Whaling Commission quota of 450, he felt that the company and the Australian Government hadn't put their hearts and minds into the industry. They'd gone off half-cocked, he thought. If they'd gone about it the right way they could have made Carnarvon the base for a great whale fishery.

He still believed this.

As they bumped out over the potholed, sand-covered bitumen road, towards the old whaling station, Fraser was expounding.

"The Humpbacks and Sperms are still out there. And so are the Blues, when they're migrating. They just didn't look for them properly. They didn't try."

The chemistry of adventure, of being involved in operating the station, of catching a whale, of proving it could be done, was beginning to have its effect. But Burton was still sceptical. "Look I had a young bloke on the Star a couple of years ago, working on his university vacation." He turned to Harris. "You remember young Hale. Nice bloke. Good worker. Caught a lot of crays that year. Anyway," he turned back to Fraser. "He seemed to know a bit about whales, including, if I remember right, that Humpbacks and Blue whales are protected around the world because you blokes killed them all off. How do you know they're out there?"

"I know mate, believe me," said Fraser. "And that protection. It's all horseshit. The International Whaling Commission. It says what's protected and what's not and how many whales you can kill. Listen, they haven't heard of the Australian Constitution and free trade have they?" he asked rhetorically, knowing nothing about the Constitution except that he recalled a vague reference in it guaranteeing the right to trade freely. "There are plenty of whales out there. The ocean isn't going to miss two. And the Whaling Commission and the Government aren't going to hear about it anyway. Listen. Nobody in Carnarvon is going to know. Look how far out of town the station is. Nobody except me goes near it these days. Even the company's forgotten it still owns the place."

Burton wasn't terribly worried about whether he was bending a law. He couldn't see anyone in authority worrying about them bringing in a couple of whales and processing them on the quiet.

Fraser was so emphatic. He'd been in the industry, worked in it and was deeply committed to it. Even if that commitment was a little blind, Burton thought, he'd be inclined to believe Fraser.

"Tell you what, mate," said Burton. "We'll have a look over the station. If that looks all right and the sums work out OK and your mate in Perth tells me he's a definite buyer at a definite price, we'll have a go at it."

"You little beauty," yelled Harris.

Fraser smiled and nodded.

A week later the Gascoyne Star, an insignificant white and rust speck on an endless sheet of Indian Ocean glass, was bathed in that soft pink light of dawn that comes as the sun explodes up through a bank of dark clouds on the eastern horizon.

Almost two hundred miles west of Carnarvon her engines stopped. She began to drift northwards to where the cold water of the West Australian Current mingled with the warmer tropical water and eventually dissipated along the equator to become the South Equatorial Current.

And then Burton saw it off to the left of the ship. Just below the horizon. A puff of white that disappeared almost at once.

Since he'd taken the Gascoyne Star to sea again, he'd become very enthusiastic about the project—more so, in a disciplined way, than Harris. Unlike Harris, for whom the only object of the exercise was to reap quick riches easily, Burton had developed a sense of mission. The idea of making big money in one short operation appealed to him. But the importance of that had diminished against the catching of a whale. "Harris," he bawled from the wheelhouse to the cabin below. "For Christ sake get out here."

The white puff appeared momentarily again. There were three more, each a little smaller and harder to see than the last. Then they stopped. Burton yelled, squinting at the horizon. "Harris. Get up here. Quick."

Harris saw them too this time as he clung to the window sill at the side of the wheelhouse with one hand and made fitful grabs at the waist of a pair of grubby jeans that wouldn't stay up. He blinked into the pink and golden light and squinted in the direction indicated by Burton's outstretched arm.

They watched for fully twenty minutes. Burton reckoned there were three whales. It had been easy to tell there were two because he'd seen two spouts at once. And then, too soon after they'd disappeared but too early for them to have re-surfaced, there was another. They were all about the same size as far as he could make out.

4

Musco, his father and pregnant mother, had echolocated the
Gascoyne Star some time earlier when the boat was many miles
from them and now, as the diesels roared into life, they knew, from
five miles away, that the boat was now moving towards them at
a fair pace. They were able to pick up its vibrations and use these
in constructing a picture-image. Musco and his family were able
to 'fix' onto the ship by sending out a series of clicks at different
frequencies specially attuned to locating and picturing objects both
near and far.

Having determined that it was about five miles away by an initial
echo survey, they then concentrated their clicks at the frequency
that would most clearly describe something in the water that far
away, and spaced the transmitted clicks so that they would not
interfere with the returning echoes. These in turn formed a total
picture of size, shape, structure, speed and direction. All this was
done at a rate of many clicks a second—not through the blowhole

or mouth but rather from inside the head. The responses were received through internal listening systems, one called a melon, in the forehead, which both transmitted and received, and another an oily substance in the lower jaw. Both of these sent the sounds to the inner ear for transmission to the brain.

There was a time when whales could call up images in this way over hundreds of miles, but now ships rumbling back and forth across the oceans too often blurred the picture, interfering with the signals.

The picture Musco's family received now, so close to them, did not make them alarmed, just cautious. Cautious and a little curious.

In a burst of chatter they decided to swim more closely together than usual. But they did not feel a sense of panic and from recent experience felt assured that trouble was unlikely.

Musco's father set a cautious eight knots. He knew that, even though they were in the peak of condition, they could only maintain their top speed of around 20 knots for an hour, at most two. If there were to be trouble he wanted them all to have reserve power to keep it up, since many ships could pace a Blue whale at top speed. The ships would always win through endurance. They could maintain their speed for hours on end, never tiring, while the whale eventually slowed, exhausted and could not take breath quickly enough for a long, deep dive before the ship drew alongside.

These thoughts kept Musco's father alert. Musco wasn't unmindful of them but he tended not to look at the potential threat very seriously. He had not been chased but he had an idea that, even if no other Blue whale could, he could beat any killer ship.

Musco knew he was special. Not in any arrogant or supercilious way. He just knew that there were things he could do that other Blue whales couldn't. For a start, his father was a giant, one of the best, and yet the family thought Musco would be much bigger than he—up to two hundred feet in length. And then there was speed: Musco could outdistance his father without much effort, with plenty of energy in reserve. Musco loved the exhilaration of bursting from a drifting start into great speed, reaching perhaps 25 knots in a very short distance, while his father and mother were still all but drifting —and doing little else but flailing their mighty flukes at the water. This was no competitive thing to Musco. It was the realisation of what he could do with his enormous being. He loved the surge and turbulence he could create. And he loved the great splash as he crashed sideways back into the water after a great leap, completely clearing the water, while most others of his species couldn't clear much more than their heads from the water, even with tremendous effort.

He'd have loved the challenge of physically outdoing a ship which had such a great reputation for endurance and speed, quite apart from its more gruesome reputation in the world of whales. But he had great respect for his father's wisdom and satisfied himself with the fantasy of winning a game against the ship, eluding it in a chase.

The family cruised onwards and over several hours noticed that the ship hardly changed course and would, eventually, if continuing in the same direction, intersect their route—some miles ahead.

Musco's father was no alarmist. But his first suspicions were aroused when the ship suddenly roared into life directly off to his right. It shouldn't have done that. He should have heard its engines earlier, approaching gradually, and become conscious of its movement that way. Had it been his family that caused it to move, and if so, was it hostile? Or was it going to be like one of those ships that whales occasionally encountered where strange small boats, rather like flat baby whales with small churning engines instead of tails and flukes, came over the side to play. The people on those boats often carried strange black boxes up near their faces, were sheathed in thick black skins and sometimes even tried to swim with the whales, by grasping a dorsal fin. That was amusing.

But it was more than amusing. Because, even though there was no sound exchanged that either the men or the whales could comprehend, there was genuine communication: and warmth. If ideas weren't specifically exchanged at the time Musco's father encountered these people, nevertheless there had been a mutual understanding that neither meant harm to the other, that each was respectfully curious about the other. It was an experience that had taught him that all men did not mean harm to whales. And that they had the means to explore the world of whales while whales had no means of exploring the world that so obviously existed beyond the sea. Musco's father, reflecting later on this encounter with men, had regarded it as a compliment to the whales that men had placed themselves at such obvious risk, in an environment that simply wasn't their own, to try to communicate with whales. And the incident was added to Musco's store of knowledge.

He did not, however, allow that encounter to lessen his wariness of the ship that was now quite close to intersecting their course.

Musco's father hoped—and the hope was so strong that it inadvertently became vocalised on top of his less demonstrative forms of direct communication—that the ship carried people who were not hostile.

That hope of his father brought the first real doubts Musco had about the ship. Musco felt the signal was too tense: it wasn't hope, it was fear. And Musco knew it before his father made it apparent by vocalising it.

They tightened their grouping. Musco just behind and between his parents, swimming in the turbulence of their wakes. His father to the right between his mother and the closing ship.

Musco's whole body quickened and intensified in its function as he fought to control his movement through the water, to keep his pace down to that being set by his father.

What if men had come with their weapons? Would they all die? Would they spare his mother and the unborn baby?

No. Men don't come to kill Blue whales and we're Blue whales, he thought in forced confidence. They'll be friendly, want to communicate like those people his father once encountered. Perhaps they'll just watch: perhaps just follow for a while and leave us entirely alone, he thought.

Between them they knew that each was straining to the limit to control their heightening emotion.

Musco's father was thinking strategy. If there was to be trouble, he was telling his mate and Musco, he would take the brunt. And that could give the others time to escape, to sound and breach far enough away while the people on the ship were still battling him.

He was aware that his mate could not sound deeply without risking the unborn calf.

Musco knew that too. And he had decided that should his father be lost, the unborn calf had to be given the chance of life. They changed course, veering away to the left from the ship.

Musco hoped it wouldn't follow.

It did.

MUSCO

Musco hoped again, suppressing the fear that was beginning to rise in him, that it would not be hostile.

The ship was alongside them now. It was a blurred shape which came into sharp focus in the minds of the whales when *all* the sensory messages it transmitted were processed: blurred vision, corrected for the refraction of light through the ocean's surface, echoes and vibrations.

Musco didn't see the ship in the same way that a human would. But his eyes contributed to the sharp picture that he assembled in his mind. They were admirably built for their purpose and their inter-relationship with his other sense facilities. Very much at the side of his head, they could not produce stereo vision, but were less under attack from the constant friction of salty water rushing past them. Their window was unusually thick as an added protection against pressure as well as the rush of the sea and they were oiled constantly by a kind of tear gland to ward off the salt water. Inside, to compensate for poor underwater light, Musco's pupils could open much wider than a land mammal's eyes, and he had a spherical lens which grasped all available light and concentrated it into a very small but very bright image on the retina which transmitted the image to the brain. All that was assisted by the oval shape of the eye which brought the retina closer to the lens so that weak light wouldn't dissipate easily. The entire internal surface of the eye was covered with reflective material, much like that in a flashlight, to further illuminate the image.

Musco combined this monocular visual picture with the echoes of the ship, produced by its noisy vibrations in the water so that he knew it perfectly as it ploughed up the flat ocean.

Musco sensed peace in himself and his father for the first time in an hour. He was beginning to feel there was no hostility in the ship. He had time to realise as it cruised alongside them that he was almost as big as the ship, and his father was bigger than it.

The tension eased. The family now believed the ship would eventually leave them, unharmed. Musco felt a shudder of relief that was partly his and partly his parents'.

They swam easily now, quite near the ship, until their tightened nerves and muscles loosened, which took a long time, especially since they had been so taut for so long. Now they breathed easily. There was no urgent huffing. They took casual gulps of air and swam just below the surface in an even, easy motion. Ten minutes on the surface taking five or six blows and ten or fifteen minutes below the glassy water.

The ship didn't leave them, though.

It stayed with them, through the morning till the sun was directly above them in a harsh blue sky. Almost at noon Musco noticed a flurry of movement on the ship. The steady, even pace, the quiet harmony between ship and whale, was suddenly disrupted. There was an urgency about the movement. Musco perceived, quite suddenly, something sinister.

Musco filled his lungs for the dive his father ordered. They wouldn't go deep but they would stay down as long as they could and try to lose the ship. In ten minutes they were a mile away and blowing hard, sending white spouts thirty feet into the still, hot air.

As they filled their lungs again the ship was gaining speed. There was a growing roar from the engines, a more forceful thrust through the water.

The ship was not going to leave them.

They sounded again and widened the distance between them and the ship. But it was now drumming louder and louder and rushing more urgently through the water. As they quickened pace so did the ship.

This would be a chase.

Musco was confident he could keep it up all day, if necessary, but he wondered how long his parents could. And how long the ship could. It had to stop sometime, he thought.

For two hours they kept a rushing rhythm as the ocean cleaved around them and surged past to disintegrate into a turbulence of air bubbles behind. Then a crash to the surface, five massive gulps of air and an arcing back below the surface. Their hearts and lungs were pounding. But Musco was sure the ship would crack before any part of his body gave in to the sustained, driving exertion.

He might have been confident in his body, but he now knew they were swimming for their lives.

His thudding heart felt a momentary emptiness, a feeling of desperation, when he realised his mother was nearing her limit. The calf inside her was almost ready for birth and weighed close to two tons. And for all her strength, and all her own weight and fitness, it was an enormous handicap in a swim for life.

MUSCO

Musco pushed himself a little harder and drew alongside his mother. He dropped a little, placed his broad, flat upper jaw just below her flipper and unleashed a monstrous effort to help her along. His father was doing the same but having a harder time of it.

They wanted to sound deeper but it would have killed the unborn calf.

They must have changed course fifty times during this dive, but still the ship was hard on them and now, as they tired, it began to narrow the distance between them. Musco's body ached but he knew he still had much in reserve. His father was beginning to weaken noticeably.

The ship drew almost alongside them.

Musco's mother, her lungs burning and the great weight of her baby tearing against every effort she made to swim faster, could hold her breath no more. Her will to live, to save the baby, was thwarted every way her mind turned. There was no escape. She had to have air.

She made to breach.

Musco went with her, on her left—his father went with her on her right. The dull sheen of the surface was close now, shattered and distorted off to their right by the sound of engines and the twisting stir of the propellors. Musco felt his father give a sweep of his flukes which shot him upwards, spurting ahead of the others in what seemed to Musco an inappropriate game of racing to breach.

He exploded through the surface just ahead of Musco.

Musco surfaced in time to hear a crack. A few seconds later he heard a thud.

The harpoon smacked into his father's arched back and penetrated through two feet of blubber exploding in the centre of his body, tearing and smashing every vital organ with splinters of metal. Almost before he realised he was hit, Musco's father was blowing blood.

Musco knew his father would die.

He had no time for grief. He realised his father had suicided to protect him and his mother, and with that realisation, Musco determined that the mother and unborn calf must be saved at all costs.

He led his mother off to the left, away from the spreading blood. His father had sounded but too much was broken. He had just the

BLUE WHALE

power for a last sad farewell to his family before involuntary nervous shuddering and flailing overcame his torn body.

Musco and his mother swam for an hour, stunned by the enormity of what had happened.

They shared their grief in a way that was total, unspoken, communication. They swam far and fast, away from the ship, which had now stopped to preside over the final agony of Musco's father. And it took the full hour for their bodies to recover slightly from the physical stress of the chase and the death.

Much later that afternoon, they were still trying to comprehend the sudden, awful gap in what had been a continuous, lifetime span of happiness. Musco was recalling some of the treasured moments with his father, those times when he first knew his father was proud of him for his skills, for his speed through the water, the day he happily conceded his superior acceleration. And of another time, not so far back in his life, when it first dawned on him that among Blue whale families the bonds were more than pragmatic, there was a spiritual love, a relationship which he hadn't been able to understand until now, when he knew a part of it had been ripped away with his father's death.

The mutual consolation between mother and son was snapped by an awareness that they were being chased again and that the ship was almost upon them. They had been so engrossed in their own shared thoughts that they hadn't become conscious of the ship until it was close.

They sounded. But Musco knew his mother was still near to exhaustion. She hadn't recovered from the morning and he was sure another exertion like the first chase would kill her and her baby.

Musco became furious. After the senseless killing of his father, the people on the ship wanted more blood, and he was enraged by their arrogant greed.

He sent his mother on.

He blew hard for twenty minutes while she raced away. And then he sounded, deep, five hundred feet down. He waited. Growing more tense, his muscles tightening, his mind concentrated on one object.

The ship was drawing closer. Now it was passing overhead.

Musco unleashed his last reserve of power. Every muscle was straining to the limit and if it was hurting he didn't notice it because his mind was too intent with fury and hatred. Even 200 feet down in the shadowless twilight Musco seemed to rip the water apart, leaving it in curling, swirling shreds of foam trailing behind him.

As the barnacled hull of the ship's bottom got closer Musco braced himself for the impact. He didn't consider the possibility of his own death. There was nothing but the destruction of the ship. It would not be allowed to take another whale life.

The ship rumbled closer. Musco was now a monstrous one hundred and fifty ton, eighty foot torpedo of destructive power, aiming directly at where the ship would be in three seconds.

Just then it lurched to the left. Instead of taking the impact full on the centre of his back, the last third of his tail scraped almost ineffectively across the hind keel of the boat, scouring deep incisions all the way back to the flukes, opening up the fine skin to reveal white blubber. The ship had only been jolted Musco knew with a desperate anger as he arched back into the water.

He was agile and powerful but the momentum of the effort was too great for him to turn in time to reach his mother.

The harpoon gun cracked again and before he could swim across the bows of the ship to be at her side, to shield her, his mother was blowing a mist of blood. She didn't fight it at all. She just lay still on the reddening water.

In Musco there was nothing left, only emptiness. He nuzzled close to his mother, comforting her, stroking her with a flipper.

5

"For Heaven's sake," yelled Burton, incredulously, "it's trying to hold it up. Trying to help."

Harris, in the wheelhouse, couldn't hear him.

He too gazed in amazement at the dying whale and the other which seconds ago had tried to ram the ship, now nuzzling it with a gentleness that seemed impossible for its size. And the huge flipper softly, gracefully moving back and forth through the blood that was flooding down the side of the dying whale.

The harpooned creature began to flurry, beginning with a trembling that shook and stirred the water into a creamy pink foam. The other whale gave a flick sideways and was gone.

Burton was still staring, bemused by what he'd just seen, when Harris shouted, "She's nearly gone. Get the dinghy over."

Burton whirled from the harpoon gun and sprinted back towards the wheelhouse along the narrow woven steel catwalk that connected the pulpit with the wheelhouse, about six feet above the deck. Harris had brought the Star to a halt as close as he dared to the dying whale, now threshing uncontrollably in the water, rearing its head, then tail, which crashed onto the surface with a deafening slap. It seemed to be trying to sound but did not have the strength. He followed Burton down the vertical ladder to the deck and aft to where the dinghy was slung in a davit over the stern.

As Burton clambered into the dinghy, Harris began to lower it, controlling the power winch with one hand and feeding the plastic air hose—provided by Fraser—out with the other so that it kept pace with the descending aluminium boat.

As the dinghy hit the water Burton threw open the shackles that held it to the davit, grabbed the 9 horsepower outboard with one hand, and snatched at the starter cord with the other until the motor blurted into action.

It was going to be pretty tricky work. The only part of the whale still moving was the tail, the flukes making weak, spent sweeps from side to side across the surface. Burton wanted to be close, but far enough away to avoid being smashed by any final flurry of the tail. And he also did not want to tangle the air hose in the propellers of either the dinghy or the Star.

He headed out directly from the stern of the Gascoyne Star, taking the air hose with him, and then he began to arc back in towards the whale, on the left of the ship.

There was no movement in the whale now. All life had gone. She rolled to her left and lay absolutely rigid, a fin reaching stiffly upwards. Burton gingerly manoeuvered the dinghy, watching the air hose all the time. He had to work quickly.

"They had to have a better way of doing it than this," he muttered to himself, cursing that he had taken on the whole exercise and cursing his ignorance now that he saw the amount of blood in the water, and confronted the reality of killing.

But he hadn't survived the day to day life he'd chosen by throwing in the towel when blood was spilled. There wasn't much romance in what he was doing and he wasn't doing it with much style, but there, in the middle of the Indian Ocean, he was whaling, chasing whales, on the basis of what he'd learned from Fraser and plain nous. He'd relied on the latter for most of his life.

"At least the weather's held," he thought. "A puff of wind in the middle of all this and we'd turn over into the drink, and lose the lot."

BLUE WHALE

Burton now had the dinghy alongside the corpse and it pitched and slithered against the whale in the still water as he stood and struggled with one of the two ten foot long hollow lances Fraser had made before they left Carnarvon.

The gunwhale made a sound like a stick run along a paling fence as it stroked the deeply pleated grooves of the whale's crop.

"Nothing romantic about this," he grunted, heaving his weight against the lance. It hardly penetrated. There was a lot of blood. And Burton was beginning to see the reality of his involvement. He had kept at it for the money and because he'd started with the project and wanted to see it through.

"Damn. This just isn't going to work." He tried again with the lance but he couldn't get it to penetrate more than a few inches.

He hadn't been able to make the lance break through that barrier of tiny blood-vessels and oil rich fat that made up the thick blubber layer. Not on the first whale. And now not on this one.

He'd had to be ugly and practical to inflate the first and prevent it from sinking and now his pragmatism overcame his desire to try to be a purist, as much as he remembered purity from the books about whaling. Fraser had told him the lance should penetrate the belly. But this one just wasn't sharp enough, or he wasn't using the right technique. It wouldn't go in.

He cursed Fraser, and edged the dinghy along the whale's cream coloured belly, now awash with blood-pink water and darker blobs of broken lung tissue that had been carried out through the blowhole in the dying moments. He kept close to the whale till he came to its anus, steadied himself and plunged the lance in.

Burton coupled the hissing air hose with the connection on the lance and air began to flow into the whale's body. The internal organs had been shattered so effectively by the blast of the harpoon that air would fill what had become just one big cavity inside the whale. He reckoned the whale would remain buoyant for the tow back to Carnarvon, two days at most.

While the whale was inflating, Burton manhandled the dinghy farther along the body towards the huge flukes which were now roughly vertical—one completely submerged, the other curving up out of the water.

As the belly inflated the whale began to roll slowly, upside down. In a short time it came to rest, sulphur belly facing the sky, the water gurgling and slurping as it lapped against the folds of the pleated crop. Now, with the dinghy positioned inside the vee of the flukes, which were splayed out on top of the water, Burton realised just how immense they were—a couple of feet on either side bigger than the ten foot dinghy.

He muttered continually as he grappled to loop a length of chain twice around the tail. He worked quickly, to race the sun as it dropped towards the sea in the west. Half submerged over the side of the dinghy he passed the ends of the chain across each other below the tail and then brought them up either side and over the flukes, tied them temporarily with a rope and headed back to the ship's stern to pick up the cable Harris was feeding out from the other reel of the winch.

It took another half hour in fading light before he'd securely shackled the cable to the loop of chain around the whale's tail and disconnected the air hose.

Harris wound in the hose and Burton nestled the dinghy into the stern of the ship, directly beneath the davit.

Later, in the wheelhouse, Harris drank from a can of beer and stared at the silhouette of the lifeless body of the whale drifting, two thirds submerged, its belly bloated by the compressed air, just astern and still a little to the left of the Gascoyne Star. Burton had fallen asleep before he'd finished his first beer.

"Cheers," said Harris raising the can. "You're a little goldmine," he said to the whale. "And not so little at that."

Musco had never been alone. He wasn't frightened. His mind was too flooded with the grief of losing his parents and the calf that would have been born. For a moment a little while ago he would have welcomed the ship a lot closer than it was now. He'd have tried once more to destroy it. And then he thought he wouldn't. He'd have wallowed on the surface, inviting them to take him. But now, late at night, he wanted to survive.

As he swam, sure in the belief that the ship had had enough blood,

BLUE WHALE

Musco decided that he must now, more than ever, procreate, in honour of his parents.

He was sapped from the physical exertion of the day, and emotionally desolate. Musco's sadness permeated out into the waters but no Blue whale heard him.

Musco had never felt this way and even when he'd got close to it, worrying about a departing brother or sister in the past, there had always been his parents with whom to share the feeling, to ease the pain. Now it was bottled up inside him. He was letting it out in heaving cries. But expressing it was very little help because there was no reply; no whale shared it with him. He took a little comfort in sharing his grief with the ocean.

Musco kept close to the surface, swimming just to stay afloat, making very little headway. He rested. Playing and finding a mate would have been the dominant thoughts in his mind now had not the ship gouged its ugly path into his world to rob him, needlessly, unbelievably, of his parents. But now Musco set his mind to work trying to put together the pieces, to try to understand the loss.

He knew that all people in ships were not malicious. Only those with the weapons. If only they'd been able to detect the weapon on this ship before it was with them.

If there were some people on ships who killed and others who didn't there had to be a distinguishing reason. His own behaviour code made it hard for him to comprehend maliciousness, until today. As he had charged the ship, he suddenly recognised he had felt an impulse he had never known, an emotion so alien he hadn't known it was buried within him—hatred. He hated that ship for what it had done, what it sought to do. And now, having regained at least some physical and emotional equilibrium, he found it difficult to understand the feeling again.

Had he wanted to destroy the ship because it was destroying *his* life? Or because it had destroyed his father's? Had he been in a rage of vengeance? This was another concept which came to him with difficulty. Or had he been enraged because he needed to be in that heightened emotional state to summon the effort to protect his mother?

These concepts—hate and vengeance—had not consciously crossed his mind before. Yet they must have been there latently awaiting the time when extreme circumstances would provoke them into activity.

He decided that, as with whales, there were different types of people. Some of them killed whales. He couldn't think of any other reason for killing them than that people needed whales for food. Which made him think how barren their world must be compared with the oceans, when they had to risk entering an environment in which they were helpless without their ships and harpoons, to find food. Did the world of the humans not have the abundance of the ocean? And were there so many people that they needed to kill so many whales to eat? Were they simply callous killers, impelled by greed? Or was there some need other than food?

Musco wrestled with these unfamiliar thoughts as he pushed through the night's soft equatorial water, his exhausted body half asleep and aching with the physical emptiness of loneliness and grief. And he felt a contempt—contempt more than hatred, though there was some hate too—for people, animals which might have among them such callous, blood-lusting individuals.

But he was young and fit, and he had an active, rational mind. He felt better as the sun's rays lit the sky.

Musco began to think about his own immediate future and it was dominated by one thing: he must carry out his plan for finding a mate this season. He would build a family. And it would be a family much the wiser for the encounter with the ship and its people.

Burton scanned the golden rim on the sea in the dawn light. He and Harris had taken watches during the night as they headed, by Burton's navigation, back to the place where they expected to find the first whale they'd left buoyed by compressed air. It would have been impossible to relocate had not Burton come up with a brainwave.

He'd pinpointed the problem back in Carnarvon, going through the logistics of the project, and come up with an ingenious solution.

BLUE WHALE

From an acquaintance in the weather station he had cadged a balloon, the sort that meteorologists use. As best they could, they had spray painted it orange to enhance its visibility. Fully inflated from a small bottle of gas it was about ten feet in diameter and attached to a 30 foot line tied to the dead whale's tail it had become a permanent orange coloured spout which would be as easy to see as any living whale.

The Gascoyne Star moved slowly and she was awkward to steer with the great weight off-centre, astern of her. Burton reckoned that the second whale would add to the weight but balance things up so that she'd move more easily.

Alone at the wheel, with Harris snoring spasmodically on the bunk behind him, Burton was haunted by the sight of the second dying whale being nuzzled and comforted, stroked, by the third. He'd always regarded whales as just big fish and, like any others, fish there for the taking, there for the convenience of man to use as he wished. Nothing to contradict that conventional philosophy had ever crossed his mind before. Now the sight of those two whales had sparked new insights. They had been like two people, one giving comfort to the other in a moment of great crisis.

He had fought hard to suppress the guilt he felt when the second whale was very near to death and he was in the dinghy. He had heard a long, mournful grunting cry—an eerie monotone, a melancholy song. It hadn't come from the whale's mouth, though, or the blowhole. It was as if it had radiated from the whole body. He hadn't heard a sound quite so mournful, or sad before. And now he was sure it was a farewell between the whales.

Burton didn't suppress the guilt now.

"Most animals make some sort of noise when they're dying," he said quietly to comfort himself. But he knew he was right about the farewell.

His reflections were interrupted—again by the demands of the job he'd started and would finish, no matter how guilty he felt now. He spotted a black speck directly in front of the ship, just visible below the horizon. He aligned the boat towards it and increased speed now that he had a positive destination in sight. Soon he could make out the orange colour of the balloon.

Heaving to near the whale was tricky and it reminded Burton that it was going to be even more so bringing the two of them into the whaling station. But he'd overcome that when he came to it, he thought confidently.

With a hundred and fifty tons of whale in motion behind, you couldn't come to a full stop. At dead slow on his dial Burton made a sharp turn to the right and stopped so that the whale in tow made a very slow pass behind the boat with a slow-motion whiplash action. Burton then eased the boat forward to gently take up slack on the cable before the whiplash climaxed and ripped the stern out of the boat. Delicately, he repeated this until he'd brought boat and whale to a stop.

Altogether, stopping the boat and securing the second whale took the best part of three hours. But they weren't working at any speed. Now they had two whales in tow, one about half a body length behind the other. Burton reckoned it would be easier than if the two tails had been side by side and bulldozing through the water. This way, one would ride in the wake of the other and drag less on the journey home.

6

Days and nights passed and Musco grew stronger in his resolve to build a family. The water grew warmer and the current was helping him swim towards the Chagos Archipelago, just to the south of the equator and west of Sri Lanka. It was a place of wonderful memories, a family playground.

With good fortune, Musco reasoned, he would not be alone in seeking out those beautiful waters. His family had encountered other Blues there in past seasons. Here he would find his mate. The great Blues were not gregarious and, in their long migration they had little time to linger in one place. If they did choose to linger they would select a location like the waters around Chagos. There was a warm ambience about the place, and food, occasionally, if he felt like it. An enveloping serenity about the water on the still days when the breeze dropped to a zephyr, before the trade winds began their endless rush. Days when a great whale could take on the pleasant rhythm of half hour naps every few hours through the day and spend much of the night conversing with the sea—or other whales —and play by moonlight on the still surface.

On one such winter several seasons ago Musco had befriended a Humpback, one of a number sharing the Chagos waters with Musco's family.

Musco loved the long and beautiful song of the Humpback. Parts of it were only for other Humpbacks but even though Musco's song was vastly different—much lower in pitch and more monotonous —he understood much of what the Humpback was communicating, especially the expressions of happiness with the ocean, and the joy in the growing friendship between the two whales.

A true friendship between these members of different species had developed and Musco was surprised at first at the extent of the affinity he felt for this whale which was so different in appearance and in physical capabilities. But there was a strong common link —their whaleness, and the almost spiritual manifestation of their physical facilities.

Through that winter as they played and rested and exchanged thoughts through song and action, Musco and the Humpback shared their whaleness. At the end of the winter Musco knew he would be prepared to die for the Humpback and the Humpback for him. The bond had not weakened even though Musco had not met him again.

Now Musco decided to wait until he was close to Chagos before he began to call for a mate. Because it would be in the waters around Chagos that he would find the mate he sought—one who liked the things about living that he did. But before he began the soft lowing calls that would tell a female of his species that he sought a mate Musco perceived, far in the darkness, the faintest sound.

His senses sharpened.

Through the still night water Musco picked up a long unbroken call, superimposed by a much higher pitch of more abbreviated clicks. It was a Blue, some thirty miles to the north and a little behind him. She was alone and seeking a mate.

He returned her call and changed course to intercept her.

When he first approached her, Musco was apprehensive and kept his distance. Their conversation was hesitant, like that of nervous humans thrust together at a school dance—Musco the gargantuan, well developed athlete and budding intellectual,

BLUE WHALE

lacking the self-confidence of manhood. She perhaps a little more self-confident but unsure of the situation, where it might lead.

In staccato bursts they exchanged information, volunteered each to the other, awkwardly.

Nika had been one of a large family group of five and this season puberty had dictated that she leave, to find a world of her own in the ocean. Like Musco's her family group had spent the Antarctic summers feeding on krill in the southern thaw and as the sun and the food disappeared they'd headed north to the equatorial waters, to luxuriate, to make love, to give birth before turning to their endless circular route south again.

This season they had taken a more direct course than usual towards the placid warmth near Chagos which was, in common with Musco's family, their turning point in the migration—the climax of their winter season. With her in mind they had made a more leisurely pace than usual in order not to waste her stored energy, so that she'd be at a peak when reaching the northern-most part of the voyage. To do so they'd headed almost due north west, from Antarctica, ignoring the aid offered by the West Australian current. The family had parted around the latitude of Malagasy, Nika going on further north, the others branching due west, intending to linger off the African coast until it was time to begin the return.

The conversation came more easily now. They swam closer together, though Musco was careful not to touch her, which was difficult after so many years of touching his mother and father. Now though, he settled for vicarious touch as he savoured the turbulence she created.

Musco was by far the bigger of the two, some fifteen feet longer, with more growth to come.

Nika soon realised she was swimming with an extraordinary male, not yet fully mature but already as big as most other Blues. At maturity, she thought, this Musco would be the biggest Blue whale she had ever encountered. She found this appealing, like his shape. Just a little vainly Nika had always thought Blue whales the most handsome creatures in the ocean and this one swimming alongside her was a fine example. She absorbed all the strong sensations she received so clearly from Musco, who now swam so close to her. She admired the grace and power of his movement, his rhythm. And she reflected on the set of his head, the way it thrust powerfully

forward and down from his blowholes to the fine line of his tightly closed jaw. The line of the jaw and the set of the small eye gave most Blues a look almost of smugness, but Nika noted in Musco that the smug expression was tempered somehow by an overall look of good humour. Echolocating deep inside Musco she could tell he was very fit as well. She liked this whale.

Musco similarly admired Nika's appearance. He liked the way she swam to complement his body, alongside but just slightly behind him so that both his head and tail extended beyond hers. This made Musco feel protective, his huge body enveloping hers. It made him feel strong and proud. And he could sense her admiration which made his heart pump just a little faster. He set his jaw a little tighter and that made him look happier than usual.

They swam together this way, growing closer, exchanging thoughts and telling of their families and their favourite places, for several days before Nika ventured a question about the long, white streaked scars on Musco's back, now healing well in the tropical waters. In colder water parasites might have infected the wounds and ultimately killed him, but Musco was recovering quickly.

He hadn't explained the events of that fateful day. He had avoided bringing his story up to date for he did not wish for a relationship founded on sympathy. But in the time they had swum together their links had deepened to a point where Nika's sympathy for Musco's loss could no longer be the foundation stone for the relationship. By now it would be a part of it, an expression of the sort of whale she was, and a strengthening of the attraction Musco felt towards her.

And apart from that he had not wanted sadness—his own grief which still lingered very close to his consciousness—to intrude into what should be a happy and lasting bond between two whales. She had sensed an even undercurrent of tension in Musco and guessed intuitively that it had something to do with the wounds. Until this time she had purposely avoided asking him, to save any embarrassment he might have felt. She thought them rather handsome, a little like the admiration drawn by duelling scars, and now she felt she could ask. Musco would be ready to tell her—that undercurrent of tension in him had gone.

In a way they *were* duelling scars, and she recognised that when Musco told her of his charge against the ship.

MUSCO

By the time he'd completed telling the whole story of that day, Nika was exhausted from the sheer effort of comprehending it. She, like Musco, knew of the past, but had spent her life without fear of ships, absolutely secure. She was shocked by his story, saddened for him. And sorrowful for whales. Her mind and her body swelled with an admiration, a physically wrenching sense of closeness, of belonging and wanting to belong, of wanting to share her every emotion and every action with Musco.

It happened differently with Musco, and a little later, when he sensed Nika's sympathetic reaction. Even if she'd wanted to hide it she couldn't. Every sensation Musco drew from her told him of the way she felt. And he wanted to return it.

Nika was attractive to him. She had been from their first encounter. But Musco was chastened by his experience with the ship and now felt a sense of caution which warned him against letting go of all his emotions. What if he did and Nika was taken from him? Could he bear the grief he knew he would feel? And also he asked himself several times searchingly, did he feel this towards her because of her reaction to his story? Or was it really because of the whale she was? Tender, gentle and understanding.

Musco reasoned it through carefully, desperately wanting to come to the right answer. When he did he whaled a cry of delight, a long cacophony of tones and excited clicks. And he ventured closer to Nika.

They swam, their giant bodies caressing, for all their size, in the most gentle of embraces, a soft undulating motion in almost perfect unison, as they brushed one another in their slow glide through the water.

Musco told the ocean of his happiness and with a flick of his flukes sped forward to express it with a show of acrobatic prowess. It wasn't just a demonstration of strength though: it was more an instance of child-like exuberance, a physical way to show Nika the excitement that filled his body.

At something close to thirty knots Musco shot from the still ocean like a grey–blue, rocket-powered wedge, driving his enormous body upwards into the sky. Against the blue surround Nika watched as he hung momentarily suspended, flicked to one side to protect his stomach from the impact with the water, and fell with a shattering explosion back to the sea. Musco did it again. And again, before he stopped to ventilate and regain his breath.

BLUE WHALE

Then it was Nika's turn, though she couldn't clear the surface.

She rolled on her back and smashed the water with her flukes in a rhythmic pattern with a sound so loud it would hurt a human ear. Musco matched it and they sounded together. Musco fell back during the dive to let Nika make the decision to turn back towards the surface, to let her indicate her limits. They went a hundred feet before turning. On the way up their fins touched, fleetingly, a gentle brush, in contrast with the violence of their ascent. But it made Musco surge forward, accelerating as they neared the surface, which he broke several seconds ahead of Nika and soared into the air.

They stopped playing when they were totally exhausted, which was near nightfall. They moved slowly through the still night, gently blowing, their flukes stirring the occasional streak of phosphorescence which shone brightly in the dark before moonrise.

Musco couldn't recall being happier. Neither could Nika. They swam, brushing fins and radiating the glow of mutual understanding.

There was developing between Musco and Nika a sense of permanence about their relationship, of security in their bond. It grew daily, gradually as they exchanged information about each other, down to the last intimate detail, developing a knowledge of each other that was totally shared.

They caressed while this grew, like the innocent pubescent youngsters they were. But now in the crystal water quite close to the Chagos Archipelago in the soft pink light of a dawn they sought something more, and they sought it as nothing other than an expression of their love, a deeper, more nourishing expression, than they had experienced before. Procreation was far from their interlocked minds and bodies.

There was indeed a magic quality in the water near Chagos.

7

The fiery Indian Ocean sunset ranged from a pastel blue through to the softest pink and deep purple with the bright red ball of sun dropping into the horizon behind the Gascoyne Star. Burton picked up the first flickering lights that told him his navigation was correct. They'd be in Carnarvon in an hour or so.

"Thank God," Burton mumbled to himself. The barometer and the radio had told him that a cyclone was brewing a hundred miles to the north and was moving in towards the coast just north of Carnarvon. The eye probably would miss the town but they'd be in for some very nasty weather. Burton knew he could not face a cyclone and tow two dead whales. He'd have to cut them free.

After being so close to the final moments of the dying whales, he regretted the killing. To have to discard the two mighty corpses would have been the ultimate humility for the whales and futility for him—quite apart from the loss of money. The slaughter of the whales had become more distasteful to him afterwards, when he had the time to think during the tow back to Carnarvon. Burton was still able to rationalise that this was a commercial deal, but after seeing the young whale comforting its mother in her death flurry and after hearing the sounds of death, Burton had wondered whether they weren't dealing with extraordinary creatures—that perhaps they could no longer be considered part of the ocean's bountiful harvest and had a much greater significance.

Dark and heavy clouds began rolling in slowly from the north. They obscured the stars as Burton brought the Gascoyne Star in towards Carnarvon and then north along the beach to where the aging jetty of the Babbage Island whaling station had been lit with two pressure lamps, placed and kept burning by Fraser, as arranged. The wind was already building.

The timbers of the dog-leg jetty and the slipway ramp alongside, up which whales were hauled to the flensing deck, had weathered well through decades of cyclonic battering. Behind the jetty and high over the beach, resting on thick wooden piles, the flensing deck and the sheds and machinery had survived well too.

Burton could see them silhouetted against the white of the low sand-dunes, blooming in the night light. There was also a pile of oil drums in a ragged heap near the jetty. He could see that when they needed the drums they'd have to move them, one way or another, a good fifty yards to the kettles, seal them and then somehow lift them to jetty level so they could be loaded on to the boat. Burton's confidence in the whole project was beginning to wane as he brought the Gascoyne Star in towards the jetty.

He had planned this manoeuvre carefully.

Dead slow, he brought the ship northwards towards the jetty and ramp and, in a slow-motion movement, swung west so that the whale corpses in tow whiplashed towards the platform when Harris let go the lines.

It worked. The bigger whale thumped into the jetty timbers so that the whole structure heaved and groaned. And yet again with the second impact.

Now Harris and Burton realised they had little time left in which to secure the whales to the slipway—if not to drag them up on to the twelve inch diameter logs from which it was made—before the cyclone began to make the sea bothersome. The freshening wind was now whipping waves into the legs of the jetty and swirling the water around the whales. Berthing the Gascoyne Star wasn't hard but an hour later it would have been very tricky. Burton and Harris were now poking around the station awaiting Fraser's arrival from town. "Look at the place," said Burton. "It's bloody spotless. Old, but bloody spotless."

Fraser *was* meticulous about his station, to the point of replacing rusted spikes in the timbers, of servicing the machinery so that it worked as well as it had in 1963 when Babbage processed its last humpback whale. The cable, stretching down from the flensing deck to the waterline on the slipway, showed not a speck of rust, when Burton ran the beam of his flashlight along its length.

He glanced at the clouding sky and felt the growing strength of the wind. "Well, if he doesn't turn up in half an hour we'll have to hike into town and get him. I want to get started."

"If this weather keeps coming we'll be in for big blow and if that happens before we've got well into the job we'll lose the lot. This place couldn't stand another blow like the last one. She'd just cave in. Fraser can maintain a building like this just so long before she falls in a cyclone." Burton was really talking to himself but Harris grunted agreement.

They needed Fraser and they needed to get started. Burton appointed Harris to hike into town to fetch him from the bar of the Pier Hotel. It would be a big job, carving up and 'trying out' the best part of 200 tons of whale, and they needed Fraser's expert help.

Harris had begun to walk when he spotted the headlights on Fraser's truck flashing into view around a dune. He whistled his relief and waited by the side of the road for Fraser to draw up.

"You little ripper," he grinned at Fraser. "You just saved me the longest walk of my life."

"No worries, mate," said Fraser. "What've you got?" He was bursting with curiosity.

"Two. Burton says they're Blues."

"Well for Christ sake, let's see them. When did you get them?" Fraser asked wondering about the state of the flesh. He grated the truck into gear.

"Three days ago. About two hundred miles out. It's been a hell of a job towing them," Harris lied, for the voyage back had been painfully slow, but uneventful. He was reflecting more on the uncomfortable mood Burton had been in for most of the time, rather than on the quality of the tow.

"Any problems?"

"No. They're tied up on the ramp. But Burton reckons the station is going to fall in and we'll lose the lot if we don't beat this blow."

"Crap. It'll stand up to the worst weather Huey can send. Let's have a look at the whales."

Fraser stood on the sloppy brake and stopped the truck behind the main shed, just near the annexe where he had his quarters.

He puffed hard from the effects of the afternoon drinking as he jogged along the catwalk around the outside of the main shed, leading to the flensing deck and the ramp. He shortened step as he followed the footway alongside the log ramp leading down to the water's edge where the two whales lay, like great balloons just below the surface, the cream of their bellies striped black by the shadows of the ventral grooves.

Fraser stood, puffing, hands on hips, his feet spread with the waves lapping over his boots. "Jesus Christ," he drawled, staring down at them. "They're big. Real big." The much smaller humpback whale was what Fraser had pictured in his mind and the size of the pair of Blues momentarily shocked him.

"Too right, they're big," called Burton. "And if we don't get started now we'll never get finished. This storm'll stop us in our tracks. It could rip the jetty apart with that force washing around its legs."

Fraser hurried back up the ramp and into the main shed to start the diesel generator. "I'll get this thing going" he shouted. "You blokes can haul the first one up while I get the pots on the go. Get those lines fastened to the loop on the end there." He pointed to a foot wide loop on the end of the winch cable.

Burton joined the cable and the lines on the first whale's flukes. The diesel grumbled and a hundred light bulbs flickered orange and red, then glowed white. A pair of powerful spotlights over the doorway to the main shed behind the flensing deck threw their beams across the deck and down along the slipway to the whales.

"That's more like it," said Burton, asserting himself but quite happily taking orders from Fraser who seemed to know what he was doing. This gave Burton a spurt of renewed confidence in the operation.

While he and Harris wrestled with the cables Fraser scuttled down a narrow stairway in the floor of the main shed to the kettles, the boiling pots. Fraser had spent his own money to buy fuel oil for the burners under the kettles.

Above him Fraser heard the winch begin its whine. Burton and Harris had fastened the big male and were now dragging it slowly, tail first, up the slipway. It was an eerie sight in the floodlights, a sea monster looming up out of the water. The solid logs of the slipway creaked under the dead weight of a hundred tons of whale but the roar of the diesel and whine of the electric winch drowned out the sound.

As it emerged into the full glare of the lights, the body looking bigger every moment, Burton's stomach turned with awe. He'd had no idea just how big this whale was until now, when it was out of the water. Out there in the ocean in its own environment it had been large for sure, but the perspective was different.

Fraser had surfaced from below the deck and was now alongside the whale, dwarfed by it, even when it flattened out on its side under its enormous weight. His six feet looked puny beside the gleaming corpse, which was almost double his height at its highest point. The rigid fin stabbed upwards at an awkward angle into the darkness beyond the main beam of the floodlights.

Burton began to worry that they had taken on more than they could cope with. For the first time he felt truly daunted. But he determined that having started something they would damn well do everything they could to finish it, impending storm or not.

"Right," he said to Fraser as the whale reached the edge of the flensing deck. "You're the expert. Let's get stuck into it."

Fraser was already donning one of three pairs of cleated boots he had brought from the back of the shed. "I'll make the first cuts. Show you the ropes. And Harris can operate the winch. Get these on . . . " He pushed a pair of the boots towards Burton.

Burton sat on the footway alongside the ramp in the bright light just in front of the whale's carcass. As he pulled the boots over his socks he felt the strength of the wind on his cheek, a cool gusting breeze from the north west, which meant only one thing—a cyclone.

"Right. Let's see if we can beat this damned storm," he grumbled at Fraser.

Fraser still claimed confidence that the aged buildings he so

lovingly tended would withstand the worst cyclone. In his heart, though, there was a fear that, if the storm was bad, the station would be wrecked.

"If this blow is going to be as bad as you reckon what are you going to do about the Star? She'll break up the jetty and the boat'll wind up high and bloody dry on the beach," he said, diverting attention from the state and strength of the station.

Burton had overlooked the Gascoyne Star in his determination to see through the scheme. Getting the carcasses butchered before the storm came was all he had thought about since berthing. He cursed and had another sinking feeling.

"We'll get started first." He hated the prospect of having to waste valuable time. But Fraser was right about the boat's chances when the cyclone came.

Fraser was now atop the carcass and had clambered awkwardly forward clutching a long handled flensing knife, one of many which he had for years sharpened and kept oiled so that the steel blade glistened in the bright light. The knife in his right hand, thrust upwards into the night sky, his left hand clutching the fin, he stood in a grotesque parody of the hunter and his kill.

Burton tried to see what he was doing but all he could see were Fraser's buttocks and back bobbing up and down as he worked the knife into the sleek skin and deep into the snowy blubber. He and Harris watched for a few minutes before Fraser told them to attach one of the lighter cables, on which swung large blunt hooks, to the heavier winch lead cables.

After twenty minutes he called for a hook and Burton, tucking it under his arm, began his first assault on the carcass. He was surprised at the firmness of the flesh under his feet and also at the ease with which he could cling to the shining skin, digging the cleats into it with each deliberate step.

In those few minutes Fraser had, quite expertly to Burton's eye, cut a deep incision into the blubber, about two feet wide. At right angles to either end of that cut he'd made two more, running four or five feet back towards the tail of the body. He stabbed his flensing knife into the body and it stood there, like a long-handled shovel in the ground. Sitting down on the whale and pushing his feet into the first cut he parted the fatty layer sufficiently for Burton to wedge the hook into the blubber, which was about eighteen inches deep.

BLUE WHALE

Fraser signalled for Harris to take up the slack on the cable and begin a slow, gentle haul. As the cable tightened and the winch did its work Fraser burrowed into the blubber as deeply as the knife would reach to part it from the flesh below.

In times of full production in the past they would have used an overhead gantry and a system of pulleys and ropes to temporarily hold the huge strip of flesh that was beginning to come away from the corpse like the skin off a banana . . . to hold it in place while the hook was reset at a stronger point on the strip. In its absence Fraser dug into the opening gap, his back against the wall of blubber, and held it apart with his feet while Burton grappled with the hook to reposition it.

The wind whined and spurred Fraser on. He followed the lifting blubber, lashing out under it with his flensing knife, helping the tearing action by cutting between the flesh and the blubber.

Burton was surprised at the ease with which the flesh parted and in a short time they had on the flensing deck a fat strip of blubber, a couple of feet wide, up to a couple of feet thick and some thirty feet long.

While Burton and Fraser slashed it into chunks about two feet square, Harris used a long handled hook to drag the blubber across the flensing deck to a circular hole. The chunks went through the hole and fell to the bottom of the first pot, now well and truly heating. It would take about forty tons of blubber but Fraser's plan was to half fill both pots to keep the boiling time down to a minimum and work them alternately.

They worked quickly and with hardly a word. By midnight the first pot was half full and cooking when Fraser closed and sealed the lid so it would do its job like a giant pressure cooker, turning the blubber to oil.

They were exhausted and Fraser and Harris were thankful when Burton called a rest so that he could move the Star to safer waters alongside the town jetty. She'd be better protected there from the full force of the weather.

"Pick us up in an hour," Burton shouted, as Fraser on the jetty, and Harris on the Star let go the lines.

All of them welcomed the break from the whale, though Burton cursed at the time wasted. He rationalised: there now seemed no doubt, looking out at the weather from the pitching bridge of the

MUSCO

Gascoyne Star, that the cyclone was building up and would hit Carnarvon with full force some time early the next day. It would gust up to eighty miles an hour and more, tossing small boats clear of the water and ripping great slabs of iron roofing from buildings.

Fraser was waiting for them as they came in alongside the jetty and he helped them with extra lines to make the ship secure. He had a vacuum flask of coffee and a pack of corned beef sandwiches wrapped in newspaper on the seat of the truck. Burton and Harris relaxed and ate as they drove back to the whales.

By dawn the wind had become a howling gale that rattled the iron roof of the shed and whipped up waves that broke over the groaning jetty. They had secured the remaining whale to the slipway and hauled her body up the ramp as far as the first whale's torn carcass would allow. But at least half her length was still in the water, the heaviest half, and the force of the wash around the jetty and slipway crashed her constantly against the piles—twice with such force that Burton was sure the jetty would collapse into the sea.

They worked on, aching and exhausted.

Burton felt it was a losing battle, that they were going to lose the station and the whales to the cyclone. Quite apart from the weather, they'd run into trouble by wrongly estimating their efficiency, which wouldn't have been such a problem if they hadn't had to race the cyclone.

They had tapped off only one run of fats and put them through the centrifugal separator. From that run they'd filled only five barrels and sealed them. But there'd been no time to move the drums up to the main shed where they could be stacked for shipment later.

The stew in the second pot was ready for drawing off when they were still running the remainder of the first pot through the super-d-canters to separate solids from liquid before running the liquid again through the centrifugal separators for more oil. They had never intended to retrieve solids and just as well because they had vastly over-estimated their ability to handle the process. The butchering stopped while they attended to the machinery.

Burton's determination was weakening. Harris was spent and demanding that they abandon the exercise. Only Fraser was still asserting they'd overcome their problems and that it was still worth pursuing. He kept reminding them of the money, but to Burton and Harris that now seemed a broken dream.

BLUE WHALE

The wind was gusting up to sixty m.p.h. and Burton thought it would get worse. Heavy rain was now blowing in from the north west and the waves were getting monstrous, slamming into the jetty and slipway, curling through the timbers which swayed before their force.

The men stood standing, sheltered from the full blast, in the doorway of the shed.

"There's just no way I can get up there and work," Fraser said. "I'd be blown off before I got halfway up his back."

"Or blown over and on to the point of the bloody knife," said Harris in a defeated, macabre tone of voice.

"All right." Burton was trying to look realistically at their plight. "All we can do is pray that it doesn't get any worse. Forget the whales. We'll concentrate on unjamming things down below so we'll have a bit of a clearer go when the wind eases off."

"If it eases off . . . ," Harris sulked.

As he spoke a massive wave crashed through the jetty and lifted the second whale clear of the slipway, smashing her through the wooden fence on the southern side and leaving her huge weight dangling over the side of the slipway into the water. The cable which secured her now angled at 45 degrees across the slipway, cut into the head of the first whale, and was bearing almost all her weight.

"Christ!," shrieked Burton. "Either she snaps the cable, or she rips the bollards out. And both ways we lose her. Or she pulls the bloody slipway to pieces and we lose both whales and the bloody building."

His lightning analysis of their situation was perfect.

Only her flukes, held by the taut cable, remained on the deck of the slipway. The rest of the whale swung drunkenly in the surging wash, one moment crashing against the pilings, and the next heaving at it as the corpse swung out with the sea.

Another big gust and they retreated further into the shed. Above them a big sheet of iron roofing was beginning to flutter in the wind. Only one sheet needed to go and the rest could follow. There was only one place to be when that started to happen—under the heavy wooden floor of the flensing deck, down with the boilers.

The heaving and pitching and the weight of the female became too much for the slipway. It sagged to the leeward side and the still vast but disfigured bulk of the first whale shifted with it. The old slipway began to break. Now the first whale rested heavily against the tail of the second, dangling in the surf. That was too much for the cable; it snapped and the flukes of the dead female slipped into the sea. The partly butchered whale slipped after it and took more of the structure with it. Now it swung about in the surf like the other, but much closer to the main shed, snapping timbers as the waves flailed it about.

Burton grabbed an axe from the tool boxes and, in what seemed like the last fury before defeat, swung it high over his head, held it there a moment, glanced at what was left of his whale, then brought it down heavily on the cable.

"To hell with it all," he said, leaving the axe where it fell. He headed for the stairway to seek safety with the others under the deck from the rest of the storm.

The three of them slept on the hard floor in the thick heat of the room below the flensing deck, secure in its shelter, physically exhausted. Burton was emotionally drained, too.

Later that day, when the wind had eased, they walked along the beach to where the whales lay in the surf, corpses kicked by waves.

Harris said: "That's an awful lot of money just washed up there. Down the bloody drain."

"Damn it," said Fraser. "Just damn it."

Burton stood there, staring, with tears welling in his eyes.

8

In the weeks since they'd met, Musco and Nika spent their time at play and making love. It had been for both of them the most idyllic time of their lives.

Musco certainly had no idea, though, that it would be like this. He'd known the bond of family—and known the depth of despair when that bond was broken—but this was something different and exciting. It was the genesis of the family relationship, his own family. But while it was just the two of them it had a freshness and unfamiliarity about it that made it mysterious.

Was it the way she looked, or the way she looked at him? Was it the sharing? Musco puzzled about it at times but could not quite grasp any single thing which adequately explained it for him. He just knew that Nika was the one Blue whale in the world with whom he wanted to share the rest of his life.

In the late September warmth they swam with the south-east trade wind. Musco had a plan for the long journey south. They had to return to the Antarctic to feed and the journey could not be delayed. But it could be prolonged in the most comfortable places. He knew if they headed west now, riding with a very gentle push from the sluggish North Equatorial current as it fanned out in a southerly sweep, they could linger near the islands north of Malagasy, savouring the warmth of the water at the southern end of the Somali Basin. Then they would pick up the faster flowing Mozambique and Agulhus currents, which would carry them south and sweep them into the southern currents for the home stretch.

His father had taken the family on this route many times and Musco had loved it. Now he knew where he wanted to go, the route he wanted to follow, and he acted accordingly. There was no conscious process involved in finding the way.

There had been no need for Musco to tell Nika what he had in mind, for communication between them was so strong there was no need for direct expression. The growth of total involvement between them had eliminated it.

Nika's agreement with the plan was felt by Musco in the same way. Direct, tangible communication was hardly ever needed between them. But Musco needed it in an encounter they had with a stranger, in the deep but small basin just north of Providence Island, between the Seychelles and Malagasy.

In the distance Musco and Nika picked up a faint call of distress from another Blue. It told them the whale was old, some 50 years, and that it felt frail and was alone.

The old whale had signalled only distress. He had not sought help from a particular plight, but wanted the spiritual help of company —sustenance in the knowledge that he could share his existence at that moment with other whales. Musco replied, revealing that he and Nika were sympathetic to the old whale's distress.

They had been hard at play, and their activity in the water probably had been detected by the old whale, prompting him to signal.

They blew deeply, recovering their equilibrium from the exertion of the game. They weren't sure whether to go. Nika's flukes flicked first, just ahead of Musco's, in response to a mutual decision to offer more comfort if it was wanted.

Within an hour they were circling the old whale, about a mile from him, but he offered no contact. And there was no reply to

BLUE WHALE

their offers. Musco and Nika knew he was there in the breeze-ruffled water but they made no attempt to go closer except to make a more elliptical movement around him. They did not go closer than about half a mile.

They did this for an hour when Musco stopped abruptly, feeling a movement at last. The old whale had sounded. They waited. There was turbulence below them and behind them and they wheeled to face it.

The old whale came hurtling up towards them and they knew he was going too hard for a veteran but they knew, too, that he was expressing his pleasure at their presence. It took the old whale a long time to recover from the exhuberance of his dive and rush to the surface. But he swam with Musco and Nika while he did.

He had been reluctant to reveal himself to them when they first approached. Blue whales usually kept to their family and, while he had warmly accepted Musco's first expression of sympathy, he was concerned that he should not impose himself upon them. The old whale had wanted company desperately. But he had waited until he was sure that Musco and Nika wanted to share with him and soften his distress. Musco detected that his heart was functioning spasmodically and that movement came painfully, his old bones wracked by arthritis.

The whale had been alone for several seasons and now, knowing his time had arrived, he had come to a place of happy memories to die. He had chosen this place because of its warmth, its peacefulness and its contrasts—the contrasts offered by the small abyss which dropped through the ocean floor. Here he could relive his happiest times, swim in the echoing depths one moment, totally unrelated to the world at the surface, and the next, become a part of the shallow sparkle of water only a few fathoms deep.

Here he would wait till his heart stopped and he would plunge, lifeless, through the depths into that unknown, darkest part of the ocean. At the last beat of his heart he would be completely content.

Musco and Nika were happy to stay with him.

The old whale swam slowly, blowing at quite an unrhythmic pace, which made Musco feel awkward. They swam with him until, quite suddenly, he broke the link between them: there was absolute silence. They couldn't penetrate his body with echolocation, though they sensed its presence.

MUSCO

Musco and Nika stopped swimming and rested on the surface, blowing in the gentlest of zephyrs. They waited at least an hour. Then from far below them came a long, mournful, undulating moan. And silence again.

Musco didn't feel the same as he had about his parents. This time it was a sense that pervaded his body in a much more gentle way, without the sharp bitterness he felt in the loneliness after his parents were taken. What he felt was only partly personal, at the death of a whale he knew. By far the strongest, almost overwhelming feeling was one of loss to the ocean, to the whales' world.

It had lost the majesty of the old whale.

But there would be others to take the old one's place. Musco and Nika, for a start. And they would make a baby and begin a family. Musco's sense of survival strengthened. He had seen four whales die this season, counting the unborn calf. He and Nika would not die, certainly not until they had been replaced with young.

Nika knew that Blue whales often make love for three seasons or more before they conceive, but she had a feeling that their lovemaking had been especially beautiful—and productive—this winter.

Inside her, motherhood was beginning to stir.

They had left the old whale and the deep, knowing that it would always be a special place for them, and headed south through the Mozambique Channel. Nika began to grow certain that she was pregnant.

Musco felt it too.

But he also began to feel the emptiness of hunger and when they emerged from the lee of Africa into the cooler water and patches of floating weed of the Southern Ocean's West Wind Drift, they put on more pace.

It was hard work swimming, with their reserves of nourishment all but depleted. The urgency of hunger kept them at it. For the rest of the journey east and a little south they would have the help of the cool current, battling against only two or three small Antarctic counter currents. They were very much aware of the ache in their tired and weakening bodies.

The water got colder and their bodies, though fatigued, still functioned perfectly: automatically their body temperature adjusted to compensate for the outside cold of the water. In the tropics their

BLUE WHALE

bodies had adjusted to the warmer water in several ways. They didn't eat and thus produced less calorific heat from the chemical breakdown of food. They were also aided by the fact that since most of their insides were watery, heat escaped much more easily into the ocean than it would from a land mammal into the air— about a hundred times faster, in fact. Large amounts of body heat could also be released through their spouts, and let loose through the skin on the fins and tail flukes which had more surface and less weight than other parts of the body.

Now, as they swam into the colder water in the south, reverse processes began to take place. The blood vessels close to their surface layers began to close up so that blood did not circulate close to the skin, turning the blubber envelope into a sort of insulating wet-suit. Heat lost through the spout was more controlled, and the arteries taking warm blood back out to the surface, tended to warm the colder regions near the blubber so heat generation requirements were minimised. Soon they would eat the protein rich krill, a warming process in itself since while being digested proteins release almost half as much heat again as fats and carbohydrates. But now their automatic systems and the sheer exertion of the swim into the feeding grounds kept them warm.

Side by side they swam at a steady ten knots, resting only occasionally and briefly. Their immediate destination was the Ross Sea, where the Ross Ice Shelf crumbled into the ocean and dumped its chunks of iceberg.

As the sun brought light, life came to the cold waters. The pack ice of the winter began to break up and the ocean revealed to the sunlight the microscopic phytoplankton that began their miraculous growth. In the icy sea the sunlight of summer was the spark of life: where the eastbound Antarctic currents ran alongside and against the westbound and where the cold water mass met the warmer sea of the subtropics, at the Antarctic Convergence, the constant surge of water swelled and stirred up life supporting nutrients from the ocean bottom. Oxygen and carbonic acid churned to the surface and, under the sun, photosynthesis spawned the single-celled plants called phytoplankton. Musco knew that at this moment, half blown, half swimming through the water with him and Nika, were tiny shrimps, which would mass in countless millions to feed on the pastures of phytoplankton.

MUSCO

Krill, or *Euphausia Superba*—at two inches, the biggest of all these shrimps—whetted Musco's appetite. They would come across the first masses of krill in the Ross Sea and their first, small, meal for half a year. From there, they would make a leisurely swim east through the drift ice. They'd pass the crags of permanent ice between long stretches of rocky coast with its amazing green summer lichens before reaching the richest concentration of krill in the Scotia Sea and the Weddell Sea around the Antarctic Peninsula and South Georgia.

And there they would spend the summer.

There they would find acre upon acre of krill gorging on the proliferating phytoplankton, so thick that they would color the sea red brown and block out light in the water below them. This was the only grazing that would ultimately ease the torment of hunger. They needed to replenish after the winter fast.

So they swam east.

At first they found only a small field of krill—perhaps a couple of hundred yards at its widest point and three or four hundred yards long.

Musco held back and allowed Nika to graze first.

She dropped her lower jaw and began to gulp water just below the surface at the periphery of the krill field. Her black baleen plates made a thick curtain of feathery bristle fibres which hung about three feet from the skin covering the roof of her mouth. This curtain ran around the edge of her upper jaw and enclosed her mouth so that as the krill soup flooded into and out of her mouth the tiny crustaceans were trapped among the fibres.

There was a time in the nineteenth century when men chasing whales could pay the cost of an entire killing expedition with the so-called whalebone, the baleen, from one or two whales (the fourteen feet long baleen of a Bowhead, for example, fetched close to $10,000), such was the demand for the stuff of fashion, corsets, and of horsewhips.

Nika—and Musco—had a much better use for it: it was their tool of life, the sieve which extracted their food from the water. Around the edge of the krill field Nika gulped a thousand gallons of ocean at a time and the constant flow of water through the baleen plates, deposited the food in the mesh and passed out at the pivot of her jaws. When the plates were full she would stop gulping. With her tongue, which was the size of an elephant, she would dislodge the food and swallow.

Musco grew impatient.

While Nika contented herself at first with the edge of the krill field, tentatively exploring the food, he plunged into its heart.

He opened his jaws wide and took great gulps of the soup, filling his mouth with water till the crop below his jaw swelled up, parting the ventral grooves so that the skin was smooth and tight, like a monstrous cream-coloured balloon. Then he'd contract the balloon, forcing the water from his mouth and ensnaring the shrimps in his baleen plates as it swirled back into the ocean.

At first Musco and Nika ate only lightly—a couple of hundred pounds of shrimp at a time. But when they reached the great shoals of krill around the Antarctic Peninsula they dined heartily, at their leisure, diving to where the greatest concentration of krill swarmed at depths from 35 feet to 350 feet. They would eat two to three tons of the shrimps—upward of five million—in a single meal.

As the season lengthened their feeding became less ravenous. And in the casual feeding sessions Musco liked to cavort. During one of these sessions Musco had his encounter with the penguin.

He had dived, mouth closed, through the krill, enjoying the strange sensation of being enveloped by the millions of tiny creatures in the eerie, red half light their presence created, cutting a swathe through them.

At a depth of about three hundred feet he came to open water below the krill, then turned, opened his jaws and rushed upwards, almost vertically. His mouth filled with water many times as he hurled himself towards the surface, but close to the top he took one more giant gulp before breaching.

For the next ten or fifteen seconds Musco stood on his tail at the surface, swaying like a cobra with St Vitus dance, helping the water to drain from between his jaws, and trapping a few hundred thousand morsels in the baleen.

As he settled back into the water to dislodge the entrapped krill Musco had a strange sensation inside his mouth. There was something there, very much alive and very much bigger than a shrimp. It was clawing and wriggling and making Musco quite uncomfortable.

He knew it wasn't unusual to scoop up foreign material when

grazing and he had never been troubled by this in the past: down it would go with the bulk of the food. But the experiences of the last six months had given Musco a new and compelling sense of sharing the ocean with other animals. While he regarded it as his ocean, he did not intrude on other animals save those which were his food, and few they were. He felt that at all costs other animals who shared his realm must be ensured the right to live.

Just below the surface, Musco gaped, allowing his mouth to fill with water and then, shaking his head like a dog worrying a toy, he spat violently.

The force was enough to dislodge the penguin from the baleen and shoot it from his mouth in a red-brown cloud of water and krill.

In a freaky coincidence, Musco's mouth had ensnared the penguin, which had been quietly pecking at krill on the surface.

Musco felt good as he noticed the indignant bird straightening its feathers with haughty little thrusts of its beak. Its dignity restored, it bobbed away with a last incredulous glance over its shoulder.

Nika wasn't very keen on this feeding method after the incident with the penguin. Musco suggested to her, however, that it was not only fun but also helped to speed the process of building and storing the reserve of nutrition on which they would live during the winter in the tropical sun.

Musco and Nika, like all the baleen whales, had no teeth and did not chew their food. Even Sperm whales, the only great whales with teeth, did not chew because they had no molars, but ripped at their food.

In place of teeth the whales had a muscular forestomach which began the process of digestion by pulverising food in an undulating contracting motion, often helped by the small pebbles and sand inside it. Softened in this way the food passed along the digestive line for processing by gastric liquids and conversion to energy and stored food. Waste passed into the intestine for a half mile journey before expulsion.

Musco often felt that he could speed the process of feeding when the krill were especially rich in numbers and succulent, by standing on his tail and enlisting the help of gravity to shake the tiny creatures down into his body.

It was energetic work, but fun. In more casual moments Musco often copied the Sei whales who grazed across the surface, trapping sea fleas as well as krill as they skimmed the rich ocean broth. Rather than gulping they set up a constant flow of water through their baleen by cruising across the water with their mouth open. For Musco it was fun to do something other Blue whales did not. If the feeding was serious he'd revert to more traditional methods.

Sometimes they would emulate the Grey whales and dive to the bottom in shallow water, stirring up great clouds of pebbles, mud, sand, crabs and molluscs with short, staccato beats of their tails, and then turn to reap the harvest. It was not just a change of diet: it provided grit for their forestomachs. They'd also look for molluscs by just nuzzling their way along the bottom, taking small gulps like leviathan goldfish.

Often they would work as a team; Musco stirring the bottom for Nika to graze and then switching roles. They were together and supremely happy. The two whales communicated with other Blues but kept mostly to themselves. They were aware of the gathering of other species in the rich water around them. They knew some of these would die at the hands of the killer ships this summer. And after the experience with his parents Musco now was not so sure that he and Nika would escape the attention of the ships as they had grown to expect in seasons past.

This summer Musco was much more cautious than he had been in the past. First, there was the killing of his parents, who had been seduced by circumstance into the comfort of believing that ships did not kill Blue whales. And there was the knowledge that this season for the first time he had no parental protection, and the responsibility of caring for Nika. He would treat all ships with great caution.

Throughout the summer Musco never lost himself completely in the joy of feeding. He was always attuned for the presence of ships and he swam close to Nika, nuzzling her protectively, when he heard one. He would relax only when he had determined that it was not on a course that would cross theirs. But even with that low undercurrent of tension, he was the happiest Blue whale in the ocean.

When he was swimming close to Nika, caressing her with his fins, he experienced an inner swelling of emotion, an impatient tugging deep inside his body, a feeling that impelled him to press against

BLUE WHALE

Nika and to feel her pressing against him in an embrace that was a reassuring expression of their love.

At times like this Musco would have to linger on the surface and sigh unusually hard, sending a column of misty condensation sometimes forty feet into the air before it was snuffed by the wind. It relieved the physical sensation, but he basked in the emotions he felt.

Musco also found expression for his emotions in marvellous feats of acrobatics.

Nika, less athletic than Musco, loved to join him in deep dives and high leaps but now she was growing protective of the fetus inside her. She would go no further than gentle spyhopping, with only her head protruding vertically from the water for minutes at a time while she followed Musco's antics.

After their exertions they would swim quietly, sharing the pleasures of impending parenthood. And while their love grew, so did they.

The constant grazing gave them energy for the moment, for growth, and for storing away for the winter. At summer's end, they had consumed hundreds of tons of food and converted it to scores of tons of whale.

Musco had always been a potentially big whale and at the end of this summer he had grown to beyond a hundred feet and now weighed well over a ton a foot. Nika was a little more fragile. And her frame was burdened by the fetus, now more than half developed, and itself weighing a ton.

In the closing days of the summer their feeding became more urgent again, as the reality of winter fasting pressed closer and they felt the need to build all the reserve they could.

By the time the sun began its slow northerly retreat, taking with it the light that fed the phytoplankton, and the plants died off, robbing the krill of their food and thus the whales of theirs, Musco and Nika had again reached their physical peak. They had defied the norms of whale fecundity by producing a fetus in their first season together; their bodies felt superb and their love was never stronger.

Musco and Nika anticipated with excitement the voyage north to their tranquil paradise, where the calf would be born.

9

Far to the north, the people of Canberra, the clinically neat Australian capital city, shivered on its high limestone plain before the cold force of a gusting westerly which came down from the snow-capped Brindabella ranges. Outside the plush-lined Capital International Hotel, huddled together around a twenty-five foot inflated plastic Cachalot and clutching placards emblazoned with the words, "Save the Whale," were a hundred or so people braving the cold to try to impress their message on those entering and leaving. They had taken up their position on the lawns outside the hotel several days earlier.

This wintery June afternoon there were more protesters than usual taking part in the dark-hours vigil because now, inside the hotel, the International Whaling Commission, the body formed in Washington in 1946 to regulate the killing of whales, was in session.

They were lobbying, demonstrating, pressing home their support for an end to all whale killing.

BLUE WHALE

In the snug warmth of the hotel conference room the seventeen Commissioners and their delegations were getting down to their first working session of the meeting, reviewing papers on world whale stocks. It would be some time before the American-sponsored motion for a ten year moratorium on commercial whaling would come before the meeting.

Before that came up there would be working papers and, after last minute adjustments had been made, discussion and voting on the Scientific Committee's recommendations would take place. These would encompass catch quotas for each country and each species, for the ensuing year, and were based on the committee's evidence on estimated whale stocks in various parts of the world and a so-called "maximum sustainable yield"—the number of whales which could be killed without adversely affecting the future of those stocks. They no longer used the notorious Blue Whale Unit (an estimate of the amount of product that could be extracted from the corpse of a Blue) to measure quotas.

The Americans had been arguing for a long time that the Scientific Committee's evidence was questionable. Along with others they pointed out that the means of measuring whale stocks, based on sightings by whale killing nations and observations from killing ships, was far from adequate. In that light, it was argued, a halt to the slaughter should be called for ten years so that, at the very least, better methods of knowing how many whales survived and how many might be harvested without hunting them to extinction, could be developed. As it was, even biological extinction, now appeared likely with some species.

Further arguments in support of the moratorium proposed that humans had no right to regard whales as a commodity of the sea to be harvested, since so little was known about them, and that there were many human characteristics in their behaviour. In an incomprehensible way they seemed to possess spiritual qualities, personal and social relationships, means of communication, and other facilities and processes, physical and mental, that were so mysterious, so great, that to kill them was an assault by puny humans on a much higher order of universal life.

The US Commissioner had worked hard to have the moratorium motion placed high on the agenda so that it could be discussed and voted on before the question of setting catch quotas for the ensuing year arose. He had been shocked by the difficulty he had encountered in persuading members that, were the American motion agreed to, there would be no need to set quotas. The opposition had doggedly argued that the Commission's first job was to review stocks and set quotas—not to consider the outrageous suggestion that a halt be called to operations.

Opposition had come in two forms: *active* from the Russians and Japanese who wanted to continue whaling at all costs, and *passive* from countries like Australia who had special resource diplomacy problems that inhibited them from arousing the ire of Japan and Russia, the two major whaling nations.

John Cameron–James, a lacklustre civil servant who had made it to the upper echelons of permanence in the Australian bureaucracy by always running with the tide, had explained to the US Commissioner quite early in the year when the agenda had been under discussion, that from Australia's point of view it would be impossible to support a resolution which worked against Japanese interests.

The United States, Cameron–James had said, had been resilient enough in its trading relationship with Japan to arbitrarily ban imports of whale products; in fact the American decision had not hurt the Japanese one iota.

But Australia was desperate to sell more beef to Japan and so bolster the failing fortunes of her cattlemen. In addition to beef, Japan was making ugly noises about her long term sugar contracts with Australia. Now Australia had iron, coal and uranium which Japan wanted—but there were always prices over which to haggle and support for Japan in the Whaling Commission was a debt which might be recalled later.

Just before the meeting he was chairing got under way, Cameron–Jones had explained further to the American that there were domestic political factors for Australia to consider. Support of the moratorium meant that she would have to close down the Point Ceta whaling station, a publicly owned company. This would cut right across the Government's ideology, committed as it was to private enterprise. At a time when unemployment was high it could not close down an enterprise that employed even a few people.

Australia sympathised with the motion, Cameron–Jones told the American, but could not support it. The Scientific Committee's figures, no matter how doubtful, were the only information the Commission had on whale stocks and Australia had to accept them and stand by the Committee's recommendations. The meeting droned on, waiting on those recommendations. Outside, things were less formal. The growing crowd of whale supporters, a half dozen television crews and a dozen or so newspaper people were being peppered with anti-whaling invective from a young woman.

Alison Debrett's soft femininity—her long blonde hair, innocent blue eyes, and doll-like nose—belied the ferocity with which the nineteen year old earth sciences undergraduate from the Australian National University could put the case for the whales. She was a great asset for the movement: her looks and eloquence made her a natural target for television reporters.

At her side, as she stood on a small rustic podium and spoke quietly but determinedly into a loud speaker pointed at the growing crowd of supporters and spectators, was Ivor Hale, her offsider in the Save the Whale movement. He was an economics graduate who had resigned several months earlier from the Department of Primary Industry, where he was a part of the team working on government aspects of the Australian whale industry. He'd grown disillusioned by the intransigence of bureaucracy and his political masters against what he saw as an unassailable case for the end of whaling in Australia and support for the moratorium. His remaining connections in the department made him a valuable source of information. Alison also found him a comfortable and constant companion.

"For those of you . . . " Alison said into the loud speaker. "For those of you who need to bring this question back to something more basic—like your own survival—there's some of that in the argument, too."

She was directing her attention to a knot of apparently uncommitted people who had stopped to listen on their way into the hotel's back bars for after work drinks.

"You breathe oxygen. So do whales. But it's very likely that the whales contribute a damn sight more than you do towards making the oxygen you breathe. They're a part of the whole system of photosynthesis in the Antarctic. The whales eat little shrimps that eat the phytoplankton—the simplest of little plants—that are virtually the beginning of life, plants that appear in the water like magic when the sunlight and the acids in the water start to work together. There's an awful lot of oxygen for our atmosphere literally manufactured in this process—oxygen that we breathe to live. There's a lot of phytoplankton, a lot of shrimps in the chain. But there aren't too many whales any more. We've let our greed muck things up. Take out the whales completely and we're probably doomed. And that's what we're doing if we keep up the killing— for things like lipstick . . . my God, lipstick! . . . and for margarine and pet food, when half the world's people can't feed themselves! We waste our time killing these magnificent creatures to feed dogs and cats . . . and for oil to grease the machines of industry. You might have forgiven the people of a hundred years ago because they *did* need most of the products. But even then, they killed the sperm whales for ambergris—the black stuff left over from eating millions of squid. They tore it out of the whales guts and used it to keep perfume smelling sweet. And they killed them for an oil so fine it did not smell when burned—the spermacetti—the substance that fills the huge volume of the Sperm's head, where all his senses are. And they killed the baleen whales for corsets and whips. Mere vanity. Well, they might have had a need . . . and maybe they didn't know better.

Today we do know better. And we don't have a need. Even in producing lubricating oil, it looks now as if we have an alternative —extracted from the hojoja plant. And do you know what people say? It will be expensive to find this alternative in a plant. And then they say that humans need the whale meat to obtain protein —but they get it by feeding whale meat to cattle in order to provide that protein!

Compare that with the efficient food chain of phytoplankton to krill to whale and it makes us look like idiots. For nothing we *really* need, we are willing to kill a superb and mysterious creature—one that may understand the universe better than we do—one that almost certainly has come to terms with his environment better than we have. After all, they've had forty million years of experience while we've been around for about forty thousand. And we seem prepared to risk the *existence* of these creatures, to impose our own young and callous hand on their being, their aged and obvious wisdom. But not only that . . . we're prepared to do it at risk to ourselves. We don't live without oxygen. We die. And here we are sticking our harpoons into a system that produces a large amount of the oxygen that makes up our atmosphere. Even if it's only for your own sake, see if you can persuade somebody today to see it the whales' way."

Alison stepped down from the little podium. Her supporters stood in silence on the grass. The drinkers who had been temporarily diverted shuffled on into the pub.

For the next two days she and Hale led the supporters in what amounted to a presence, a sort of would-be external conscience for the delegates inside the hotel. They talked, lectured, discussed, pleaded, sang, drew, listened and—whenever the opportunity arose —lobbied in support of the whale. They sold bumper stickers, lapel badges and T shirts to boost the not insubstantial bank account that Alison and Hale had built, from various money-raising ventures.

It was towards the end of the third day that Alison recognised the Japanese commissioner scuttling down the steps of the hotel, long before he should have emerged from the meeting. He was followed by a snake chain of subordinate officers. And then, behind them came the Russians in similar fashion, pursued by Cameron–Jones, who stopped at the bottom of the steps and watched both delegations tumble into cars and drive off, presumably to their respective embassies.

Hale collared a former colleague in the hotel lobby and discovered the drama's genesis—and its meaning. Neither Japan nor Russia would accept the quotas recommended by the Scientific Committee. They were far too low for both Japan and Russia and they had argued very emotionally for much higher figures. That argument had been going on when the American commissioner, having now gained sufficient support in a desperate few hours of lobbying, utilised a procedural device to halt discussion and force a vote on the moratorium. It was carried. The Japanese and Russian delegations had resigned from the Commission on the spot, effectively wrecking it.

"You know what's going to happen now," Alison said to Hale. While they criticised the Commission they recognised it produced *some* controls on the slaughter.

"Yes. And there's not much we can do to stop it. But we can do something. We can make things hard for Point Ceta. Let's go home. I want to make a call to Perth."

10

Musco and Nika had taken the long, eastward way around the Antarctic continent towards the West Australian coast, but had turned northwards earlier than Musco's family had the previous winter. They shunned the help of the West Australian current and chose a course northwards, almost through the middle of the Indian Ocean.

They were making for Chagos again, planning to spend their winter in gentle play and await the birth of the calf towards the end of the season, in August.

The Indian Ocean was swelling quite heavily and the breeze was whipping foaming caps from their tops. It would have made pretty heavy going for a small ship. To Musco and Nika it was another mood of the sea. They worked harder physically to make progress through the turmoil but they were oblivious to the extra effort. It was as though their bodies automatically adjusted to the weather conditions, just as they compensated for water temperature.

BLUE WHALE

In Nika the anticipation of motherhood had been growing steadily. She had sure knowledge the calf growing inside her would become as big as Musco, whom she just knew to be the biggest Blue whale alive. She anticipated the calf's strength and size with excitement. And the feeling grew more intense as the fetus grew. She could feel the heartbeat, detect the blood roaring through it, sense it drawing on the placental nourishment. What made the excitement for her was not just motherhood but that inside her belly was growing—she could feel it constantly—another Blue whale which was, truly, fashioned after Musco. The calf would be Musco in size and in nature. He would be gentle, loving, clever. He would become wise: a great whale.

Nika longed for the birth, not to confirm that of which she was sure, but to share her bursting love for Musco with Musco's calf.

Musco had a reserved sort of pride about the calf. Like Nika, he could virtually see it growing, sense all its features and already he knew it was a fine calf. But that was only a small part of the feeling inside him which swelled apace with Nika's belly. It was a more mellow, softer but much fuller experience than that breathless ache he felt when he thought of Nika. It was love in anticipation, expectation of his own family. The calf would be a new and fragile giant who would share their love and the richness of their realm.

Above them, the storm strengthened. The waves grew and the wind lashed at their tops so that huge sheets of water were whipped into the air before they crested. It was a full sub-tropical cyclone. For the first time Musco and Nika became fully conscious of the weather. They abandoned the surface they had been ploughing and took to a little depth, just far enough down to still enjoy the great turbulence close to the surface but so that they swam on a more steady horizontal course. When they breached to blow they did it rhythmically, in sympathy with the motion of the sea: surface in one trough for one blow, wait for the wave to pass, surface again in the next trough for the next blow, and so on, until their lungs were replenished and they'd dive again.

Once established it was a pattern they relegated to sub-consciousness.

Musco went onto a sort of auto-pilot which, with no conscious effort on his part, navigated from his memory map, orientating ocean depth and topography, salinity of the water from its bouyancy, the direction of the current and the sunlight, water temperature, and distance from land. His body was acutely tuned to all of these and sorted through them while Musco remained totally unaware of them, on another thought plane altogether.

In that rhythmic swim, enveloped in the undulations of the ocean, its fluidity streaming past his sensitised face, it was easy for Musco to become almost meditative.

He wondered at the nature of people and how the unborn calf would experience them. He recalled again how once his father had felt close to people sharing the water with him. Perhaps it was possible that those people had wanted to return to the water, much as whales had come from the land in the far distant past. Perhaps they and the whales had once been of the same big family, branching out on their separate ways when the whales returned to the water; the whales changing, learning, growing, loving their ocean, the people changing, learning, growing, loving their land. But now some people wished to return to the ocean; perhaps they did not love the land as whales loved the ocean.

Did they want to remove the whales to make room for people? Why would they want to do that when there was so much space? People had changed the existence of whales and now threatened it. Musco couldn't understand this manipulation of the whale species.

Confronted by what had happened in Canberra, with the discussion over how many whales should be killed, Musco's mind would have baulked into confusion, switched to another state.

Musco accepted killing for food. He knew the tiny krill he ate died to nourish his body. But he was aware there was a limit to the number of krill that died for that purpose—a limit set when the whales' bodies declared "enough". Enough was enough in Musco's mind and the way in which whales had died—first the Rights, then the Greys, then the Humpbacks—each being left in peace only when they became close to obliteration—did not mesh with his way of thought.

Had the people been hunting for food alone they would not have ravaged the whales, family by family as they had, till they almost disappeared from the oceans.

BLUE WHALE

Musco could not comprehend greed and his thoughts kept beating against such impenetrable barriers in his effort to understand the behaviour of the humans. If he could have been sure of his safety he would have liked to get closer to people. His father had found that there was an elusive barrier which prevented full communication between the people he had encountered but that there was the stirring of a contact of minds, something which could be nurtured until, perhaps, the barrier shattered.

He had sensed that, even though there were vast physical differences between whales and people, there was a similarity of sorts in thought—even that people were capable of great thoughts, almost like the whales. If that were so, what things they could share, with the barriers overcome? But whales lived at ease in their ocean with their companions. People had their companions, but they ventured out of their land environment into the water through the use of inanimate objects—ships—and they used inanimate objects —harpoons—to kill whales. Did they use such objects in coping with their own environment? If they did, Musco reasoned, they could not have the same capacity of mind as whales, for it meant that, in mind and body, people were not at home on the land. Nor were they in the ocean.

Each way his mind turned Musco's thoughts were frustrated. He would never understand people. Perhaps the calf would, in time.

Nika swam close to Musco, rolled on her side and swept her flukes across his back in a gentle slap that crashed through the ocean like a thunderclap. She had sensed his troubled frustration, and wanted to stop it. The slap had the right effect.

She was becoming used to the way in which Musco often lost himself in thought to a point where he began to send out shudders of anger at his inability to go beyond a certain point. She could sense when his brain was rushing with a thousand different thoughts, all coming together but not reaching as far as he wanted them to.

Nika sometimes went into this state of mind too but she stopped when she felt that she could not resolve all her thoughts. Musco frequently did not stop and needed to be brought back to the moment. She feared he would explode. Now they explored the growing fetus as they swam, and pictured Chagos, where it would be born. The tropical waters would warm the young body until, nourished by hundreds of gallons of Nika's milk, it would build a suit of blubber, thick enough to insulate against the cold when they returned to the Antarctic for his first season of grazing.

Together Musco and Nika shared pleasure in anticipating the birth, of introducing the calf to that most beautiful of places, Chagos. They would be there soon.

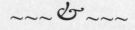

"You're mad, bloody mad," Burton grinned at Hale, stretching out his hand in greeting. "Always said you were."

Hale introduced Alison as they crushed their way through the crowded Perth Airport terminal. Burton still didn't quite believe the hare-brained scheme that Hale had outlined by telephone several days earlier. He had tracked down the Gascoyne Star to a berth in the fishing harbour just south of Fremantle, port of the West Australian capital.

Burton was always ready to listen to ideas but he'd put this one out of his mind as a flight of fancy. But young Hale seemed quite sure that he wanted to charter the Gascoyne Star for at least three weeks as a mother ship so he and a group of his friends in the Save the Whale movement could get out on to the whaling grounds and interfere with the Point Ceta operation. They proposed to run inflatable zodiacs between the whales and the catchers, preventing the gunners from firing.

Burton had harboured a regret over the incident with the two Blue whales and his sympathy in the months since that disaster had begun to tend more towards the whales. And when Hale mentioned that he and his friends could pay their way in the scheme, from the organisation's funds, Burton decided that he'd give it a go. Anyway, the Gascoyne Star was without work at the time.

Burton had liked Hale when, as a young economics under-graduate, he had helped him to moonlight on lobsters during a university vacation some years past.

"When can you be ready?" Alison asked as they piled into a taxi for the ride to the Gascoyne Star.

BLUE WHALE

"As soon as you're ready," Burton said. "There ought to be enough room on board for all of you. Twelve, right? Well. As long as you're not too fussy."

~~~ & ~~~

Just to the east of Chagos there was the great deep, the western edge of the Cocos–Keeling Basin. It was still eerie during the dawn when Musco and Nika decided to stop their purposeful swimming for the first time in a month. It was here, where they had first made love, that they had chosen as the birthplace of the calf.

For Musco there was always a great feeling of achievement when he reached his winter grounds. It was one of the two high points of his seasonal cycle and brought anticipation of good things, of leisurely play, of unexpected and luxurious feeding, of quiet pleasure and of being a great whale at rest. Now there was the anticipation of the birth.

While they waited for the calf to make its move there was Nika, and there was loving.

Musco stopped swimming. He just allowed the momentum of the eight knots pace to carry him through the clear, clean water. The water nursed him and he loved it. He was totally at rest with his upper jaw making a small bow wave which rode up over his head and parted in the gentle wash around the small hump which rose protectively in front of his pair of blowholes.

Musco was sure that, very, very faintly he could make out a sweet warm smell. There were few nerve ends around his blowhole to detect a smell and the system for carrying it to his brain was miniscule but Musco felt a new sensation in that complex brain, a new sensation that told him this place had a sweet scent.

It was more a subtle message to his consciousness that the water was good at Chagos, that it was a fine place for the calf to find the ocean.

Nika swam up alongside him from behind, rolled sideways and slid her enlarged belly along the full length of Musco's side. She turned and did it again down the other side towards his tail, very slowly. Then she rolled on her back and swam just below the surface, so that she drifted lazily, just touching Musco's belly.

Here, with the sky arcing above them, the sea sprawling endlessly around and twenty thousand feet of water below, there were no proportions. Nothing was relative, except the whales to each other. They were two beings, ecstatically joined—Nika suspended upturned just below the surface, Musco above her, his ten feet of penis slipping forward softly along her smooth afterbelly until he felt it reach the place where her body opened for him. They remained undulating gently for a few seconds, hardly rippling the surface in their movements, and then parted.

Musco swam off to one side, turned and nuzzled Nika's back, helping her to right herself and lift herself to the surface again where her spout exploded twenty feet into the air. As Nika blew, Musco continued to nuzzle her and stroke her sides, her mouth, her tail with his flippers and to pat her gently with his flukes.

Then they just lay side by side on the surface of the water, a shallow wash across their backs. The tropical sun warmed the air they breathed and that, with the afterglow of love, demanded sleep.

Through that afternoon Nika discovered something completely new, about Musco.

She had been dozing alongside Musco's sleeping body, her smooth skin slipping and softly bumping against his. She was thinking about the calf, half dreaming, half conscious.

Musco was deeply asleep, his body demanding almost total rest.

Nika was lost in her semi-conscious thoughts, in the touch of Musco's great body and in the rhythmic sound of their sighing and blowing.

When she heard the new strange sound she involuntarily flicked her tail and shot several yards away from Musco. She heard it again. A long, deep rumble, like the groaning roar of an iceberg as it cracked and splintered from a glacier.

She focused on Musco. He was all right. It wasn't a ship as she had suddenly feared. Then she heard it again, deeper and longer. It was coming from Musco.

He snored! Nika thought it a wonderful sound.

Musco and Nika spent most of their time over the deep basin to the east of Chagos. Occasionally they would leisurely swim towards the shallow water which shelved up from the depths and eventually broke the surface at the rocky archipelago. In the shallows it was always warm and the white sandy bottom seemed to give a clarity to the water.

Sometimes they played and a couple of times they fed on a school of crabs, which were a great delicacy. Mostly they just swam, and while he was often tempted to race with Nika, to put on great bursts of speed until he would be several miles ahead of her, Musco never left her side.

Nika's belly was taut, the skin and thick blubber layer stretched tightly around the two tons of fetal calf inside her. She didn't feel uncomfortable in this advanced state of pregnancy, just a little awkward occasionally. When she knew Musco would like to speed, she wished she was more streamlined so that he would sprint and she could at least try to keep pace with him, joining the game.

Soon she would be streamlined again. But still Musco would have to limit his speed because they both would have to swim at the calf's pace.

It was late afternoon and they had just crossed the point where the basin plunged away to twenty thousand feet from the shelf which surrounded Chagos, when Nika felt the first real movement. Musco picked it up, too.

For months now they had been delighted by the twitches and turns which flicked and tugged at Nika's belly. Now she felt something much stronger.

Instead of the quivers she'd felt earlier, this time Nika felt a definite pull, as though there were some mysterious force inside her with no specific point of contact but which was somehow able to tug at her body from all directions.

It was strong but it was gone in a moment. Nika stopped swimming. Musco was by her side.

She felt it again and this time the mystery was still there but the shock was not. A good feeling overcame her and she was ready for the next tug.

Musco stayed by her side, swimming quietly around her. It was so subtle that it was hard for him to detect, but he felt the movement in her belly. The pulls were quite close together now, with barely time for Nika to blow between them. She took a series of sharp breaths, blowing as quickly as she could to fill her lungs for what was to follow.

MUSCO

Musco helped her to roll over on to her back so that the upper part of her belly and her lower jaw were just above the surface, shining creamy white and rose tinted by the falling sun.

Her tail dangled at a shallow angle so that her genital slit was no more than ten feet from the surface. It was awkward and she constantly used her flippers to hold the position.

Musco supported her as best he could, waiting for the first sign of the calf's tail. To be sure he'd be ready at the first sign, he swam close to Nika's genital slit.

The calf would be born tail first to prevent it from drowning. Were it born head first there would be too long a time between severance of the placental life-support and freeing of the tail from the mother for it to get to the surface and take its first breath. It would drown.

When Musco saw the tail for the first time he controlled his excitement. He had a great responsibility. Nika kept her position and began to push. The calf came easily and quickly.

Musco was amazed that it seemed to just keep coming. Two tons of perfectly formed baby Blue whale, about twenty five feet long just kept emerging.

Musco nuzzled closely in to the calf, waiting for its head.

The moment the calf's head was free it was completely separate from Nika. She twisted, gulped some air as her blowhole broke the surface and dived again. Together with Musco, they nuzzled the calf to the surface.

For Musco it was a breathtaking moment. His senses were dazzled with excitement. It was a big calf—they had known from echolocation for a long time that it was a male. And Nika. She had done this for him. No. They had done it together. He wanted to embrace the calf and Nika. And the whole ocean.

As the calf's head broke the surface of the ocean for the first time Musco and Nika, on either side, gave it a soft nudge. It blew. A jet of vapour shot about six feet into the air. Then another. And another.

Musco felt a small flipper brush against him and turned to see that the calf was trying to swim. Then its tail flicked and the flukes moved sharply downwards. Nika and Musco had to work quite hard to hold it to the surface because, though it was making swimming motions, it would have sunk like a stone had they let it go.

BLUE WHALE

The calf had not yet breathed sufficiently to expand its rib cage fully, to give it the buoyancy it needed, and the movements were still quite frail. He would need time to grow, to put on weight—and blubber—before he would be buoyant enough to swim with the grace of his parents.

Just as it had been with Musco and Nika a few nights earlier when they made love over the basin, there was no perspective so the calf looked quite in place as a newborn baby with his parents, despite its enormous size.

They supported the twitching calf for about half an hour, booming out sonorous expressions of sheer joy. When they heard the calf try to copy them they were delighted.

They were sure now that he could swim.

Again Nika rolled on to her back and swam gently across the mouth of the calf until she felt its undeveloped baleen plates against her teats, which had emerged, one from each of the concealed pockets on either side of her genital slit.

Nika contracted her mammary muscles and shot a jet of thick, rich milk into the calf's mouth. He drank. And she squirted again. The calf drank many gallons of milk before it rested.

It was thick milk, a little like cottage cheese and enormously concentrated, so that it not only gave the calf all the nutrition it needed, but also supplied him with enough drinking water to maintain stability of his body fluids. Whales need fresh water, like other mammals, and are unable to drink sea water. They have no ability to sweat and concentrate their urine, preserving the fresh water content of their bodies. While the calf's parents used tricks like eating krill, which is not very salty, the calf drank milk which helped him. The milk was extremely fatty—about ten times fattier than the milk of humans—and had almost no sugar, so that when it was digested the fat produced a substantial supply of fresh water to the body, as a by-product.

Musco nestled closely to Nika while they shared the burden of the half floating calf's weight on their backs.

He would be called Sul.

Sul grew very quickly. He guzzled the best part of a hundred gallons of Nika's milk daily and rewarded his parents by growing almost visibly, by hundreds of pounds a day. After only a week he weighed close to four tons and was very handsome.

But he was by no means strong. He still swam weakly in an incongruous flittery way. And it would be perhaps six months before his baleen plates and his digestive system could handle anything more substantial than the oceans of milk which Nika squirted into him.

He was entirely dependent on Nika for his survival. But even in the few days since his birth he had become dependent, too, on Musco.

Almost from birth there was an emotional attachment that went much deeper than mere cupboard love, deeper too than the slow-developing reciprocal love between other baby mammals and their parents.

Sul was born with a love of what Musco and Nika were, Blue whales. Almost immediately after birth his consciousness was working, conceptualising, realising. He did not need to be told that he had come from Nika's belly, or that both Nika and Musco somehow had caused his arrival, or that in every way he resembled them both. He knew he was a part of them and he was glad of it. It was from this that Sul's special love grew. The bond between the three would grow stronger through the few days that they had left in their winter paradise.

Sul learned a lot as the season dwindled.

Some days he would lag behind Musco and Nika as they were swimming. When they were several lengths ahead of him he would swim off to the left or the right, always sure of where they were, but testing, nevertheless, how long it took them to notice his absence.

Within minutes Nika would be at his side, slap him quite smartly with her flukes and shepherd him to rejoin the family trio. For a while, despite the slaps, this was by far Sul's favourite game. Musco and Nika indulged it for what it was. But when Musco wanted it to stop, Sul knew it had to and it did.

Sul enjoyed his parents' amusement at his efforts to sound, especially when he tried to fluke—breach the surface with his tail as he went down. Musco loved giving the water a farewell slap, uncharacteristic as it was of Blue whales to break water with their tail when diving. Sul wanted to do it too. But the best he could manage was a small swirling stir, near the surface. And having dived he could manage only a few feet before having to return to the surface to blow. He was learning, though, and enjoying it as much as his parents were delighted to help.

MUSCO

For Nika, in spite of all the joys this winter had brought, the need to return to the Antarctic was becoming urgent. She wished a speedy end to the winter.

Beautiful as she was, and superbly fit when they had set out for their winter sojourn, the long fast and the drain of feeding the fetus, giving birth and then feeding Sul, had all but spent her reserves of nutrition. The occasional meal of crabs and molluscs from the desert waters had done nothing more than titillate her appetite. Now she had an angry hunger that could not be satisfied until they returned to Antarctic waters and the krill which summer would bring.

Knowing this, and the need to swim slowly so Sul could keep pace, Musco was happy to begin the voyage now. Sul had grown and learned enough to undertake the long swim.

They took a course almost directly south until they picked up the inner edge of the South Equatorial current hundreds of miles to the east of Malagasy and just to the west of the central longitude of the Indian Ocean. This would help them into the great eastward drifts of the Southern Ocean and on into the Antarctic, and food.

11

The Gascoyne Star had become a menace to the three active catcher boats of Point Ceta Pty Ltd. While Musco and Nika had gone north, Burton, Alison and Hale had gone south and had got more efficient at hindering the catchers.

Opinion polls showed that public support for the whale protesters was strong—and the financial backing that flowed in following television news coverage gave tangible backing to that support. Despite opinion, though, the Government maintained its line, working for the re-establishment of the International Whaling Commission in the hope that Japan and Russia could be persuaded to return to the fold, bringing with them some of the renegade whaling nations like Peru and Korea. Australian officials were reluctant to raise a finger that might irk Japan; such was the delicacy they saw in their resource diplomacy.

With financial backing, strong emotional support and frequent, glamorous media coverage, Burton, Alison and Hale had become a focal point. The original three-week programme of hindrance had been extended indefinitely and the Gascoyne Star was now making forays out of its home berth at Albany, almost alongside the whale station at Point Ceta.

They had fitted out the Gascoyne Star so that, while it was never comfortable, it carried a dozen whale protesters with relative ease. It was equipped with two zodiac inflatable craft and well-tuned, powerful outboards. They had radio jamming gear that totally disrupted communications between the company's spotter aircraft, which flew out in sorties fifty miles offshore to the ground and the catchers. Operating out of Albany, rather than Fremantle, where they'd begun, meant they had only to go as far as the chasers themselves to reach the grounds. They were still behind the chasers getting there. But they'd home in on one, track it down in dogged pursuit and when close enough would lower the zodiacs, to shepherd the whales away from the catchers. Alternatively they would place themselves between catcher and whale so the harpoon gunner could not get a sighting without risking killing the protesters.

The small and once peaceful port of Albany on King George Sound, with a vast, placid harbour where once humpback whales came to sing their songs, was a town divided in fury.

At season's peak Point Ceta employed some four hundred people on their flensing decks and in the factory. The company had brought in an extra two hundred anticipating that the collapse of the Commission would allow them to range further than usual, ignoring their quota. But the Save the Whale activity from the Gascoyne Star had impeded operations significantly. And at the gates of the shore factory massed pickets of whale supporters and trade unionists striking for the closure of Point Ceta harrassed every company employee, and shipment of goods that entered or left.

There were brawls in the once quiet streets of the town between Save the Whale people, or anybody who was suspected of being one, and those who considered their jobs were at risk or were being prevented from working because of the disruption.

Two hundred State police had been assigned to the town to supplement the small local force.

While Point Ceta had its problems with the Save the Whale

people, Gascoyne Star had her problems with the pro-whaling townspeople and itinerant workers. The pickets against the protest vessel were less organised, but she was subject to guerilla attacks at night when alongside the wharves. So now she moored out in the bay, coming in only to refuel, re-supply and change crew, and staying as briefly as possible. All the time she was alongside, a small division of police had to be hived off from duties at the factory to protect the ship.

Protest and outrage against Point Ceta reached a peak every other day as news came into Albany of the Russian and Japanese flotillas in preparation for the now open Antarctic season, and of Peruvian and Chilean and South Korean activities. There was news, too, of scores of small pirate operations to take whales off Africa and the Atlantic coast of South America—of plans to store whale oil until, inevitably, the market tightened and prices went higher. Clearly the immediate future would mean a market glut, but Russia and Japan had discussed their own marketing controls to ensure prices were maintained internationally.

Burton was engulfed in the cause. Occasionally when his cynical streak got the better of him he rationalised that the Star was well and profitably employed.

Alison was still the media favourite. But Burton, rough and ready, whom the newspeople thought really ought to be on the other side if appearances were any guide to a man's ideas, was getting wide exposure too. Alison and Burton frequently appeared on television newscasts together. Hale relegated himself, fairly happily, to churning out fact sheets for the media, which were more often than not ignored, in the interest of pursuing the adventures of Alison and Burton. Hale didn't mind missing the limelight but he did regret that he was no longer cast as Alison's partner, a public role which had until he'd slipped from it, helped to reinforce the private one. He was a little jealous of Burton, whom Alison found quite appealing for his gritty exterior, for his weaknesses and paradoxical moments of softness which showed through occasionally, and for the enthusiasm he had for the cause.

Burton was flattered but, out of respect for his early friendship with Hale, did little to encourage Alison. He would have liked to, though. Hale was mainly shore based, but for this sortie he wanted to be on board.

MUSCO

"I've missed out on the last three," he told Burton, feeling a little resentment at the time Burton was able to spend with Alison on board Gascoyne Star.

"All right mate. No problems," said Burton. "You're in."

It was late October when Musco, Nika and Sul passed Cape Leeuwin, the western toe of Australia. With the help of the South Equatorial they had arced across the Indian Ocean towards Australia and, once past Cape Leeuwin would be into the huge rolling swells and eastward drift of the Southern Ocean. From there they would move across the current southwards, getting help all the while to their first stop in the Ross Sea. As Musco and Nika had done last season they would make their way gradually to the richest grounds near South Georgia, once the initial hunger pain had been assuaged.

The swells were superb. Musco would rise to the top of one then flick his tail as he felt it peak and surf in the unbroken water till his momentum was lost in the trough. Another flick and he would rise again to the crest of another swell.

He'd take three swells and turn to see how Sul was progressing. The baby tried it once but couldn't quite raise the power to flick himself into the downward rush of water. So he tried again and just slipped backwards into the tough as the swell passed.

Musco came up alongside Sul and this time gave the calf a push as the swell peaked. Sul skewed down the front of the swell and then broached and rolled over four or five times until he regained his dignity. Musco watched with amusement. Nika was a little worried for Sul but saw Musco's lack of concern, and she, too felt a glimmer of humour in the situation. Such moments of lightness were rare at this stage of a migration: the need to eat was beginning to become urgent.

Musco shepherded Sul for a while until Nika caught up and they swam on as a family group finding the swells of little real help in making progress. A smoother ocean would have made things a little easier.

BLUE WHALE

Through the soft surge of the swells Musco picked up a new sound. It wasn't a sound of or from the ocean so, when he first detected it, it caused him little concern. But the hoarse, mosquito whir of the twin-engined Cessna five hundred feet above persisted and it began to irritate his senses. Nika and Sul found it uncomfortable too, and Musco wished it would go away.

But it did not. Instead it circled above the family group and the pulsing, piercing, unfamiliar sound got stronger. It began to hurt as it grated on their senses.

As they dived to try to escape the buzz above them Musco recognised the familiar sound of a throbbing ship. He tuned in for a moment. There were two, not one, and others far off in the distance. He worried. Nika would be too weak to try to outpace a fast ship if it were seeking them out. Sul, too. And Musco, while largely unconcerned about the hunger pangs in his stomach, knew that he wasn't at his peak if it came to a battle to defend his family. He felt weak and defenceless. Utterly exposed.

The buzzing aircraft followed them. Each time they surfaced for air it was there, sawing into their senses. And the sound of the two ships was drumming nearer.

Sul snuggled between his parents, aware of their concern. The grim picture, the blood, the pain, the anguish, of his parents' deaths thrust itself into Musco's consciousness and he couldn't shut it out. He could not bear the loss of Nika and Sul. It would be impossible. He shuddered.

They could sound, Musco thought desperately, but Nika and Sul probably would be unable to go deep enough for long enough to become lost in the ocean. But there were few alternatives. Musco did not know what to expect from the buzzing object above them. But he knew the never-ending endurance of a ship chasing a whale.

They sounded. Sul couldn't get past fifty feet and Nika was struggling at that depth. When they surfaced the incessant buzz was still above them and the ships were now only a few miles away.

He focused on them and devised a two-stage plan. First they would try to lose the ships by swimming erratically. If the ships still kept track Musco would stop and fight before all three of them had reached exhaustion, as had happened with his parents. While he engaged the ships, Nika and Sul would still have energy to swim on—and perhaps escape.

It meant they would have to use very short, sharp manoeuvres and there would be very little time in which to make the first stage of the plan work. Nika and Sul would tire very quickly, to a point where their exhaustion would demand surrender to the ships.

Now there was a change. The sounds coming through the water told Musco that only one ship was still chasing them. The other had stopped.

But there was a new sound. Overhead the buzzing, and through the water the pulse of one ship. And now two more noises, high pitched, much like the sound above them, but these were in the water and they were moving towards the whales much faster than the ship still in pursuit.

Musco felt his two-stage plan would have worked—even against both ships because he was familiar with their strengths and their weaknesses. But this new sound . . . he was at a loss again. Nika was doing her best to hide her terror from Sul who was now almost clinging to her with his near flipper. But such a feeling is impossible to disguise and Sul, too, was aching with fright.

What puzzled Musco was the pitch of the two new sounds. The drum of a ship was low and thudding and it was ships he knew to be a threat. The higher pitch of the two sounds made him sure they belonged to much smaller objects than ships. He stopped Nika and Sul for a moment and concentrated hard. Through the ocean and much fainter than the noise of the motors came a slap-slap sound: there were small boats moving very quickly over the water, rather than through it. And they were coming nearer with greater speed than the ship.

They were between the whales and the ship and Musco was confident he could deal with them, now that he had a picture of their frailty in his mind. He was confident, so long as they weren't carrying some new weapon, more horrible than the harpoon gun which had killed his parents.

He planned to charge them. If that didn't frighten them away he'd surface beneath them and smash them, or at least overturn them. The humans inside would be thrown out of their environment into Musco's and he would be at a tactical advantage.

BLUE WHALE

They came closer and Musco steeled himself. The ship was well behind them but still encroaching.

Musco, Nika and Sul sounded and, when they were twenty feet below the swells, flicked off to the left. They heard the drum of the ship change course with them. The slap-slap of the zodiacs and the buzz of their outboards stopped for a moment, then roared again in the same direction as the ship.

When Sul's smaller lungs were bursting for air, they breached together, off to one side of the ship. Musco had made several sharp, erratic turns with Nika and Sul right behind him, so that the ship had over-run the point at which it expected the whales to surface.

The aircraft was still overhead, watching the whales' evasive action and reporting every move by radio to the ship. The whales were more agile. But the ships had endless stamina.

As they breached, Musco got a brief impression of the horror on the bows of the ship, the cannon swinging towards him. Then one of the two small boats moved between the whales and the ship. If the man behind the cannon had been able to get away a shot it would have hit the small boat rather than the whales. Musco was perplexed. It was a feeling that niggled its way through the enveloping terror he felt for his family.

The small boat stayed close to the whales while they blew briefly and sounded again. It seemed to try to follow, but made no aggressive move. The ship drummed on and was several minutes changing course to follow the whales.

Again when Musco surfaced the zodiac was alongside them, doing nothing but quite obviously placing itself between him and the killer ship. Musco struggled to sense the same aggression he felt from the ship. It didn't come. This time the ship was in line for a shot. But the boom of the harpoon gun did not come.

It happened again and when Musco surfaced he came so close to the zodiac he could see two people inside it. In a frozen second he stared at them and their gaze was locked back into his eye. In that moment Musco sensed something strong—a feeling of oneness —between the people in the boat and himself. They were making sounds that were harsh and flat to his ears, which were attuned to the more mellow sounds of the sea. But in that clattery, alien noise he felt a note of sympathy for him and for Nika and Sul.

MUSCO

Musco realised that the ship had turned away from the whales and the small boat.

It had given up the chase and was thrumming off in another direction. The buzzing sound overhead had gone, too. But the zodiac stayed with the whales a while, fussing along the length of Musco's great body and back again and all the time Musco was feeling empathy with the boat and the people inside it.

He still kept himself between the boat and Sul and Nika. But he couldn't help going back to his thoughts at the time of his parents' death and his certainty that all people were not like those who had shot them.

Now Musco heard the other ship again. It had started and was coming towards them and he shuddered. But the zodiac stayed with them and he felt less terrified. If it could ward off one ship in this way then it could do the same again. The zodiac made no attempt to leave the whales and Musco kept his family clinging alongside it.

As it came closer it made no unexpected change of course. And its motors slowed.

Up close, Musco felt a strange familiarity with the ship. He examined it closely and, though he could not be sure, it seemed very like the one that had taken his parents. He noticed the dreadful cannon in the bow but thought that perhaps all ships carried such weapons. On this ship, though, there was no person behind the cannon. Friendship between the people on the ship and those in the zodiac was obvious to Musco, and he felt that implied friendship with the whales.

The feeling on the zodiac, Musco perceived, was very strongly directed towards the whales. Strongest in the girl. But in the man with her he could feel some uncertainty, a nervousness that might even have been fear; there was a quite distinctly heightened emotion that filtered through the overall sense of empathy with the man.

For the first time in his life Musco had felt that he could now distinguish between individual people.

Nika sounded her relief and snuggled close to Sul and Musco. She also sounded a note of urgency: she was not as confident as Musco in their safety and she wanted to be away from this place quickly. She also wanted to resume the voyage to pasture. The need to eat was making itself felt quite sharply, through the breathlessness that engulfed her now in the wake of their brush with death.

The whales turned southwards. Musco hoped that in the Antarctic the ships would leave them alone, as they had in the past.

On board the Gascoyne Star, the zodiacs stowed one above the other on the after deck, Alison was hugging Burton and Burton in turn was looking sheepish, particularly conscious of Hale's presence.

"Did you see that eye?" she was asking Burton excitedly. "Did you see it? He looked at us, stared at us. Didn't you feel it?"

"Fantastic," was all he could say, flatly.

Alison turned to Hale. "Did you see them? They were Blues. The bastards are chasing Blues. The hungry mongrels. It's the end. They'll wipe them out in one season. Don't they know what they're doing?"

She was becoming more furious and more frustrated with every word.

"We're doing what we can," said Hale trying to placate her. He had taken a fatalistic attitude. It was a hopeless cause now. But one which had to be fought.

"We've got to do more. Where's Alan?" She turned from following Hale up the ladder to the wheelhouse and looked for Burton. He had slipped away to be on his own at the bow of the Gascoyne Star.

"What's the matter with him?"

"How should I know," said Hale.

Burton had a stab of guilt. He still hadn't told Alison or Hale about the episode with the two Blues. And he felt bad about that. But he felt worse now after today's encounter.

Leaning against the now disarmed harpoon gun he recalled the whale's eye when it surfaced beside the zodiac. He was sure that as it stared at him there was a flick of recognition in that ridiculously small flat grey-blue eye.

And the white scars on the big whale's back haunted him.

12

The first great bergs of drift ice made Musco feel better. Sul was getting plenty of milk from Nika, but Musco, needlessly anxious, was sure that she wasn't producing enough to satisfy his needs. The calf had been putting on weight at two hundred pounds a day since birth—even more in the first few weeks—and was now close to fifty feet and twenty tons. But he had more to grow before he was weaned and Nika was frail now, especially after the trauma of the chase off Cape Leeuwin.

Musco was worried for Nika, too.

When they reached the Ross Sea and echolocated their first small patch of krill he held back, despite his own ravenous hunger, and allowed Nika to eat. She stormed into the krill, taking monstrous gulps and must have eaten a couple of tons in less than five minutes.

The need to eat well came not just from their depleted bodies and the hunger for nutrition. The actual process of eating itself required energy, of which they were drained, for in the cold

BLUE WHALE

Antarctic sea the krill were at water temperature and the whales burned up energy merely bringing the icy food up to body temperature, so that it could be digested. The digestion provided heat that would help to warm the food in later meals. But in this first meal of the season it was important to eat fully and well, to begin the process again.

When Nika was eating more sedately, Musco joined her. Sul was astonished. He hadn't seen this behaviour before and took it as some kind of game. His baleen had not yet developed fully. It was still little more than a mere ridge around the roof of his mouth and when he mimicked his mother's great gulps he spat out almost as many krill as he took in. A few lodged in his short plates. He didn't know what to do except to shake his head violently and worry at them with his tongue.

Some were washed from his mouth. Some passed on down his throat and for the first time he discovered a new and very vague, dull sensation—taste. Even when he was mature Sul would have only the most rudimentary sense of taste, but at the back of his tongue there were a few buds, linked to a very weak nerve. And as the krill passed over these buds for the first time they initiated a sensation that was different from that created when Nika spurted gobs of milk into his mouth. Much more readily detectable was the tactile sense of the shrimps' exo-skeleton scratching over his tongue. That startled the calf after his constant diet of creamy textured milk.

As Musco and Nika had done the season before, they ate and played their way east towards the Antarctic Peninsula and the great krill grounds, and all the way Sul was learning that to feed he did not always have to suckle.

Musco tried not to display anxiety about where they were heading. He knew they had to go to where the krill was thickest and richest, if they were to store enough food to last next winter. But he was worried. There had been the attack on his parents. And now the attempt by a killer ship to take him and his family in a part of the ocean where Blues had never before been bothered, but where there were always ships, killing other whales. He worried that their lives were in danger more than they ever had been.

They tarried among the drift ice close to the rocky shore between Ross and the peninsula. There was krill, but not enough. So slowly they moved east.

MUSCO

The Antarctic Peninsula is a rocky finger that juts northward towards Tierra del Fuego and forms a natural barrier between the seas on either side of the southern continent.

Musco and Nika had been apprehensive but they had not been prepared for what confronted them when they rounded the tip of that finger of ice and rock.

Musco recoiled. From every direction his senses were assailed by the sound of dying whales and what shocked him most deeply were the sounds of dying Blues—Blues calling for their mates, Blue calves calling for their dead mothers. The mourning cries came from far off to the east, around South Georgia, and quite close in the immediate lee of the peninsula.

Musco heard Cachalots. And where last season the death cries had come from the Fins and the smaller Minkes and from Seis, now there were Blue whale cries as well as the others. He heard Humpbacks and Rights.

The sea, which should have been red-brown with krill, was bright red with whale blood. Under the ghastly sound of the crying, dying whales came the muted throb of ship engines, and the boom of harpoon guns.

The crisp, crackle of krill that Musco had hoped to hear was drowned. He turned and blocked the way for Nika and Sul, and shooed them back around the headland, away from the sounds of death.

Nika's heart pounded with anxiety. Sul was bewildered.

Musco was outraged at the arrogance of the people on the killer ships. Ever since the death of his parents he had been unable to discover why the whales were killed and taken from the sea. Why they were relentlessly run down to the point of exhaustion, then exploded to death, pumped like grotesque balloons to stop their corpses from sinking to the peaceful depths, marked with flags and bundled together in death rafts, and then swallowed eventually by monstrous ships with gaping mouths at the stern —ships that billowed black smoke and had the smell of death about them.

He would never understand.

Musco would have been even more outraged to know that the people used what they took from the whale carcasses for decorating their bodies, for making machines run smoothly and for feeding

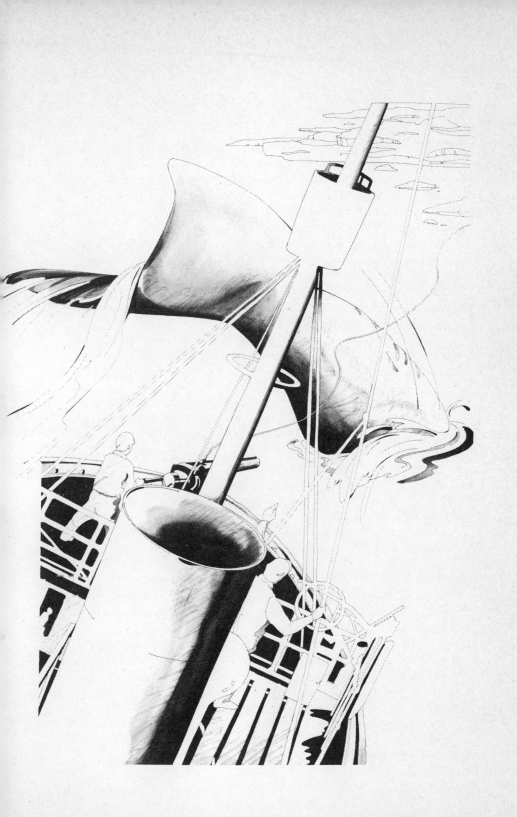

animals that were bred to die—some, like cattle, to provide food, others like minks, to satisfy vanity. And to know that the whales of the ocean were mutilated in this way because people preferred to take a whale's life, which to humans was cheap, than to spend time and money finding ready alternatives . . . Such arrogance and rapaciousness were beyond his comprehension.

Musco had arrived at the baffling conclusion, that to *some* people a whale's life was cheap. It was a conclusion he could not understand. He had felt that humans had to be intelligent, like him, and equipped with powers of reasoning. If they could build ships to serve them, they had to be. But if they had such powers Musco had puzzled, how could they do what they did to whales?

Musco had no time now for exploring causes of people's behaviour much as he wanted an explanation. Now he was more concerned about the effects of that behaviour. His urgent problem was to decide how he and Nika and Sul would feed that summer when the killer ships were poised in the centre of the krill pasture. It was a dilemma of risking death at the hands of a harpoon gun in order to eat enough krill for the winter. Alternatively, it was risking that they would find sufficient krill by hunting down the isolated patches that grew in other, less rich seas of the Antarctic.

Nika needed to graze intensely for herself and to keep producing milk for Sul and, in his first season, it would be difficult for him to eat enough in the more sparse krill fields away from South Georgia. Musco decided that the second choice was preferable. They might be lucky and find a rich patch to themselves and be able to avoid the risk of the ships.

He turned his family back towards the Ross Sea. In a week of patrolling they found only enough krill to provide energy for the one day on which they fed. Musco quickly realised that he and Nika were not building up reserves for the winter.

Sul was doing the best of the three because he was taking milk from Nika and improving his grazing technique and that, at least, was one comfort for Musco. Soon Sul could be completely weaned and Nika would have time for more grazing, and the krill she ate would be all hers, instead of being shared with the calf. But that didn't solve the immediate problem. Nika had to eat enough for herself *and* the calf. And grazing spasmodically, as they were, they were not putting on enough weight. None of them was sufficiently nourished. Musco decided they would have to risk the ships as best they could. They turned again for South Georgia.

He planned for them to find a permanent hide and graze only when the ships were well away. Just where they would hide, he didn't know, but felt they could use the ice in some way. Darkness offered no help since there was none during the Antarctic summer.

As they travelled Musco developed his plan for survival. He would hug the peninsula shore, hoping that the ships would not venture in close to the dangerous rocks and pack ice. Once through the dotted islands of the South Shetlands, around the broken tip of the peninsula into the Weddell Sea, they would look for a place to hide, close to the shore and protected by drift and pack ice.

As they picked their way carefully through the ice and islands towards the Weddell Sea for the second time this season, the cries of dying whales came again.

This time Musco pressed on. The urgency of the need for large amounts of food and concern for his family helped him to suppress his fear. Nika and Sul were not able to suppress theirs and they huddled close to Musco.

All three tried desperately to shut out the moans of agony and mourning. But they could not. They concentrated on using their senses for navigation but all the time, even when they concentrated their hardest, the sounds of death came through.

Musco pushed on, clinging close to the pack ice of the Weddell until he found what he was looking for, a narrow, east-facing entrance to a small inlet, that widened slightly past the mouth. When it was viewed from the sea at a distance of anything more than half a mile it would appear to be just a continuation of the edge of the pack ice. It would be almost undetectable. The ice was high enough so that, if they breathed gently, their spouts would be unseen behind their shelter. From there the whales would be able to swim out to graze while Musco and Nika took turns to listen for the approach of ships.

It was still risky. While they grazed they would be in open water. And they had to breathe, so they had to blow and their spouts would always be visible for many miles. But that was a risk of survival, Musco reasoned.

Inside their hiding spot they felt a fragile safety. They ranged out to eat quickly, returning as soon as their stomachs were full to rest and allow digestion. They would range out again when their stomachs were clear.

It was a fitful and uneasy way to feed. But it was safe and it met their needs.

In a month they were forced to spend only one period in the hiding spot when they wanted to be feeding and a killer ship patrolled close to the edge of the pack ice. Behind their wall of ice, Musco, Nika and Sul held their breaths to a minimum, blowing softly so their spouts would not give them away.

It was a heart stopping moment but it soon passed and they went back to their routine.

They were beginning to feel more confident. Apart from the one incident with the catcher ship they had heard nothing nearby— only the distant and saddening sounds of the ships and the whales to the north. Their feeding was regular and they were beginning to achieve the nourished condition they needed.

It was apparent to Musco that he was alone among whales, not only in his great size—now—one hundred and twenty feet and still growing—but in the decision to hide. From his father he had learned, as most other Blues had, that many years ago there had been great slaughter. But in more recent years few Blues came into contact with the ships, at least the sort of contact Musco had had the season before and earlier this summer.

Perhaps it was his size that attracted the ships to him and therefore thrust on him, through circumstances, the ability to think of evasion rather than escape. The previous encounters had sparked off in Musco a new, and uneasy, foreign feeling of vulnerability. Until last season he had always felt in command of his circumstances, supremely confident of mastering any threat.

Now that confidence had been broken and there was suspicion and mistrust.

Nika did not feel it, and certainly not Sul. And Musco was sure that most other whales had not experienced it either. He had never detected in other whales the feeling he had now. It was those whales who had headed confidently for the richest krill grounds earlier this season and had met the ships. But with Musco the ships had forced on him a new thought process, a new capability, which gave him the means of avoiding them now, rather than doing battle with them when they came seeking him out.

BLUE WHALE

While Musco and the family were feeling gradually more secure in their summer routine and becoming sleeker, they did not neglect the need for a constant monitoring of the sounds of the sea to ensure that the ships were far from where they were feeding.

Nika was keeping watch during a summer's end topping up session. Musco and Sul had been gulping down great mouthfuls of krill broth. And now Musco was showing the calf some of the finer points of skimming, which in less dangerous summers Sul would find a pleasurable means of grazing.

Nika signalled a worried caution as she picked up a sound of a ship which she felt might be heading towards them.

In his pleasure at watching Sul learn skimming Musco had breathed some heavy sighs of joy, for moments of pleasure this summer had been few. He had spouted quite high, perhaps forty feet, and Nika was frightened they may have been seen.

Musco joined Nika on the edge of the krill field and concentrated. There was no doubt that the ship was heading towards them. Sul was still happily skimming up broth and now was even making a clumsy attempt to spyhop and shake the krill from his baleen, as he'd seen his father do.

Musco called to the calf. But Sul's still developing sensory system was concentrating on the joys of feeding. He did not hear the call.

Musco sent Nika on her way back to the hide and irritatedly flicked off in pursuit of Sul, calling to him all the time. Still the calf did not hear, his head half out of the water wildly trying to rattle krill from the feathery trap in his jaw.

It was not until Musco swept right up to the calf and thwacked him across the back with his mighty flukes that Sul realised he was in danger. With Musco nudging him along, the calf began to swim towards his mother, who was now well ahead. But the ship had been closing in. It had spotted Musco's spout.

They were running for the hiding spot but by Musco's reckoning, were not swimming fast enough.

When he and Sul reached Nika they were doing the best Sul could manage—about eighteen knots—and the ship was getting closer. If they could maintain this speed for another fifteen minutes they would reach the hide. But the ship was tracking them now and it would see where they had gone.

MUSCO

Musco peeled off to the left. He was biggest; they would chase him first.

He made a fuss in the water, blowing and spouting to decoy the ship away from the entrance to their hide.

He felt sure the ship would follow him and it did.

It seemed to watchers on the ship that Nika and Sul just disappeared into the pack ice. But Musco kept heading off to the left, making for the shelf of ice that dropped into the sea. Each time he breached he blew hard, out of necessity but also to draw attention to himself. At the edge of the ice he blew hard again and then sounded. The chaser closed in.

Musco knew the ship could not come after him under the ice. But he also knew he had to surface soon for air. He began to rise slowly towards the ceiling of ice and shift towards the edge where he'd find open water and another breath of air.

The harpoon would be waiting for him to surface but his lungs were burning and he ached for air. He surfaced only a foot from the edge of the ice and sent a spout forty feet into the air, grabbed half a lungful of air and went down again. As he did, the harpoon gun boomed out and Musco felt the ice break as the explosive tip blasted into the ice only a few feet from him.

He surfaced again and blew quickly, taking long enough for the gunner to relocate him but not to fire off another shot. He then dived away from the direction of their hide and was quite deep when he turned under the pack ice to swim back towards Nika and Sul, with just enough air to last the distance. The ship headed off, following his dive from the surface searching for him in the wrong direction.

When he reached the hiding spot and surfaced gently Nika was moaning in agitation and making little dives under the ice and calling. Sul was not there. They had reached the hide safely but the young whale had panicked at the sound of the harpoon gun. He had sounded and swum out under the pack ice. Musco breathed deeply and disappeared under the ice. Nika stayed in the lagoon calling.

They could hear Sul now, calling them from far in under the ice. Musco tracked the source of the call but his echolocation was confusing him under the ice. Sul wasn't where he should have been: his call had ricocheted in the shallow water between ice and gravel bottom and broken into a thousand diverse signals.

BLUE WHALE

Musco began to sort through the many signals that glanced between ice and bottom, searching for the strongest and its source. He was frantic.

Sul would have been exhausted from his acrobatics during feeding, let alone the hard run back to the ice hide. And under the ice he would soon run out of air, with nowhere to surface. Sul would have been aware of that, but in his moment of panic would not have thought of it, so great was his terror.

Even if he could make his air last long enough to find a way out, he too, would be confused by the ricochets of his echoes and could easily swim in the wrong direction. Under the ice it would be much colder than in the hide or the open ocean and Sul's newly grown layer of blubber might not be sufficient to withstand the sudden plunge in temperature. It would be dark too, and frightening for the calf when he overcame his panic and began to search for a way out.

Musco was frantic. He followed one signal that seemed strong but Sul was not at the source. He called for Sul to keep crying out and to stop swimming.

He'd be able to follow the cries much better than the weak and diffused echolocation signal he got from Sul's presence in the water. But the cries were getting dimmer and Musco himself was bursting for air.

Sul's cry flickered. And stopped. In echolocation all Musco could feel was the presence of a small, still Blue whale, somewhere under the dark ice.

Musco, almost exploding for air, thundered inside, heaved in outrage, in grief, in disbelief. He whaled a deep scream.

Nika had heard Sul's call die away and then heard Musco and she dived in under the ice in a panic. She knew what Musco's anguished cry had meant but could not believe it. She had to go in under the ice where Musco had gone after Sul. Her mind and body were frenzied with the fear of what had happened.

When Musco, his great body sobbing inside, surfaced in the lagoon, Nika had gone.

He could hear her calling under the ice, a long deep moan. The panic had gone. Now she was searching vainly for her calf. She called again.

Musco whaled back but he couldn't move. He was too spent. Nika knew the ice and would find her way out. Sul hadn't been able to. And Sul was gone. Musco barely floated, his blowhole just bumping through the mirror surface of the lagoon, sighing, blowing deep sighs of anguish and grief.

If the catchers came now he would not move.

He was shattered.

Enveloped, engulfed by it all, it was some moments before he realised that now he could not hear Nika. She had not reappeared in the lagoon from under the ice.

He was weakened and emptied but he managed a shallow descent, rather than a dive, to below the ice ceiling and called. There was no answer. Nothing.

He tried again. And again. Until there was nothing left. He could barely flick his tail.

So complete had been his grief when he realised that Sul had gone, there was no room for more aching. Neither his mind nor his body could accommodate it. And he would not believe that Nika would not come back from under the ice. He would not allow himself to think that she had gone too.

Musco just lay there in the still water, mostly submerged, sighing and sobbing inside and lost in his emptiness. He stayed in the lagoon a long time. And Nika did not come.

He didn't feed. He hardly breathed.

He stayed still, until the sun had almost gone and he could feel his lagoon getting colder, the water getting crisp with little needles of ice.

Out in the ocean the krill had gone. The sun had stopped nourishing the plants they fed on and the long darkness was coming. The whales were leaving, retreating before the encroaching ice.

Musco wondered whether he'd stay until his lagoon turned to ice. It would lock him in and swallow him as it had with Sul and with Nika. But that was no way for a great whale to die. Not if a great whale had a choice. And Musco began to realise that he did have a choice. He didn't care for company again. He couldn't conceive life again without Nika and without Sul.

If he was going to die, succumb to his shattering loss, he would do it nobly, not allowing himself to be frozen and crushed to death in the jaws of the ice. He would die in a place where he could rejoice at least in being a Blue whale, a great Blue whale. And he remembered the tiny ocean chasm, near Providence Island, west of the Seychelles, and the old man whale.

The ships were gone now. And most of the whales. The ocean was silent except for the rush of the waves in the heightening wind of impending winter.

For the first time in a month Musco heaved his massive body and shoved himself out into the open sea. It was more a mental effort than physical. But the movement in his body gave him a small lift, feeling the buoyancy of the ocean, its life and its verve. He would never, he was sure, recover from his grief but the ocean gave him to courage to push on to his summer grounds, the place with all those memories, the place where he could relive the days with Nika and the birth of Sul. Those days of bliss when he felt his heart would burst with joy.

He went east around the gradually freezing continent and found that the pack ice in places had begun its northerly expansion and he was further out from the land than he had been last season, when he made this voyage with Nika.

He travelled past mountainous icebergs, ghostly in their stillness or slow rolling motion against the sharp pitch of the sea.

At Prince Edward Island he turned north, completing his second circumnavigation of Antarctica in two years, and made for the West Australian coast. He would try to ride the current and this time he'd go closer in shore where it was strongest. He hadn't the motivation for a hard swim.

13

In the fishing harbour at South Fremantle, in the wheelhouse of the Gascoyne Star, Burton ran his finger softly through Alison's long blonde hair, and in a circular motion across her smooth skin, warmed by the morning sun streaming in through the window. She murmured a soft grunt of pleasure.

"Who'd have ever thought those rough hands could be so sweet," she said.

"Yeah." He paused. "We mightn't have won the war for the whales. But at least I got you."

"You didn't *get* me," she said reproaching his chauvinism. "We got each other." She paused. "And I'm glad."

For the Save the Whale people the war had been lost in the midsummer of that year. At Point Ceta, despite the protests and the fights and the hampering operation of the Gascoyne Star, the catchers had kept dragging in whales of all species and sizes.

The company had defended its action as survival and a national

BLUE WHALE

effort for Australia, so that if the slaughter begun by the Japanese and Russian fleets and the marketing agreement between those two countries had meant a cornered market for whale products, Australia would have its own supply, for a while at least, from Point Ceta.

The slaughter had toiled on and by the end of the summer even the most conservative of the Japanese and Russian scientists had declared that for commercial whaling this had to be the last season. Not a species, north or south of the Equator had escaped the uncontrolled, almost hysterical onslaught of whalers.

More than a hundred thousand whale carcasses had been accounted for, before counting stopped.

In the north and in the south the Japanese and Russian factory ships had been serviced by freight shuttles, bringing supplies and taking off the whale products as fast as they could process the slaughtered whales.

The scientists declared that this season must be the last, that the stocks of all great whales, Blues, Humpbacks, Cachalots or Sperms, Greys, Minkes, Bryde's, Seis, Fins, Rights and Bowheads, had been slashed so severely that it could be predicted with great certainty there would not be enough whales for further commercial exploitation. With their particularly low fecundity, there simply were not enough whales to reproduce at a rate which would maintain the order. But most people refused to believe such alarmist "nonsense." There would always be whales, even if, this season, by mistake, they had killed too many, they said.

The main thrust of the protest had dissipated when the army of Save the Whale groups around the world realised that their war had been lost, despite small victories in many battles.

Burton and Alison had kept operating the Gascoyne Star out of Albany until their funds for fuel and supplies were gone and the flow had dried to a trickle as the futility of it all became apparent to their supporters. Hale packed up and went back to Canberra and the Australian National University, beaten by the whalers and by Burton.

By late January, Alison and Burton had stopped trying and returned to Fremantle. Harris had felt—rightly—that he was crowding things on the Gascoyne Star and disappeared quietly to find another job.

And Alison and Burton were now going to keep the Gascoyne

Star going as a coastal tramp, moonlighting on lobsters. Their emotions had run the gamut when they finally admitted defeat and now they were reconciled to it, saddened and a little embittered and fully resolved to allow the carelessness of man to run its course. There was nothing they could do, they felt, except care for each other.

Alison got off the bed and, standing on her toes and reaching upwards, stretched her lithe brown body, soaking up the March warmth that streamed in through the glass.

"You get the coffee going and I'll make the toast," she said, reaching for the lower half of a bikini that hung from the top spoke of the ship's wheel. "Turn on the radio, could you?" she asked through the cotton tee-shirt she was pulling over her head. The last line in a news story caught her attention before the newsreader moved on.

" . . . a museum official has identified the giant as a Blue whale . . . The Minister for Primary Industry has announced that the bounty on superphosphate is to be extended . . .

"What did he say?" she asked.

"Something about a Blue whale. I guess someone's seen one," Burton said. "That'll be novel," he added sardonically.

Alison had to know more. She left the ship and walked along the jetty to the fishmarket which was abuzz with business. She asked two people before she discovered that early that morning a great Blue whale had been discovered stranded in the shallows of Leighton Beach, just a few miles north, on the other side of Fremantle Harbour's river-mouth opening to the sea.

She came running back to the ship.

"Alan, we've got to go. The whale is stuck. The museum people say the only thing that could pull it off the sand is a tug but the Port Authority says they're sorry but it has a busy schedule and shipping—of course—must come first."

"Al, we could try to save it . . . " she pleaded.

"For all we know it could be the last Blue whale on this earth . . . the last whale even," she said dramatically. "The Star's got the gear and it should have the power."

Burton nodded.

~~~ & ~~~

BLUE WHALE

Nika had swum for days along the edge of the pack ice in the Antarctic, calling for Sul and for Musco. She had patrolled back and forth along its ragged line, calling for Musco and listening for his reply.

He hadn't heard her because she was so close to the ice that her calls had reflected out to sea or had just broken up and dissipated beneath its edge—bouncing between the ice ceiling and the shallow sea bottom. The calls had not penetrated the lagoon where Musco had just waited in utter despair.

Nika, grief-stricken, had eventually resolved that Musco too had been lost with Sul. But she would not accept it completely. If there was the slightest chance of survival there was one place that Musco would have gone and that was Chagos, the place of their happiest memories. She had set out for the place of their first love-making three weeks before Musco had made a move from the icy lagoon. But she was disheartened, despairing that, even though she might make it to Chagos, she would never find Musco again.

Moving up the West Australian coast, exhausted from her grief she had suffered what to her was the final indignity inflicted by man on the ocean.

She had surfaced in a thick patch of crude oil that had been discharged by a ship illegally blowing its tanks and had inhaled a huge gob of the filthy, clinging, stinging liquid.

It was burning her lungs as it passed into her system. And it was slowly suffocating her from inside. It was too much for her in her broken state of mind.

Nika gave up. She would end her life quickly on a beach rather than suffer the agony that the crude oil was inflicting. It wasn't so much the oil, though, as her broken heart and spirit. The oil might not be fatal, in other circumstances; her lungs were huge and physically she was strong. She might have felt able to recover, at least enough to make it to Chagos. But the inner strength wasn't there without Musco and Sul.

She had turned east and run herself into the shallows, and she now lay gasping unable to move. She would either crush the life out of herself by her own weight when the tide receded, suffocate as she pressed down on her lungs, or, unable to move in the shallows with waves washing over her blowhole, she'd drown in a soup of water and oil.

Nika moaned. Calling out. Crying, just as the old whale had in his last hours.

She was unaware of the crowd gathering on the beach. About fifty yards of shallow water, channeled by rips, separated them from her.

A few surfboard riders had paddled out but had cautiously kept clear.

She lay there, crying her heart out. Her spirit and will to live were gone. Her life was ebbing with the tide.

The board riders edged away when they saw the Gascoyne Star moving in towards the stranded whale. They were cautious but curious and hung back.

Alison took the wheel while Burton lowered a zodiac over the stern and began to tow a cable in towards Nika. Inside the zodiac was a length of four inch Manila hawser, eye-spliced at each end.

"Come on you blokes, give us a hand," Burton called to the board riders.

It was obvious what he was trying to do.

Burton wondered for a moment, when he got close to those massive flukes, whether the whale would flurry and bring them crashing down on him and the zodiac. But she was lying still, immobilised by her own weight, and Burton put the thought out of his mind. He manoeuvred the zodiac into the vee of the flukes and recalled to himself that he had done this before.

In the small chop, whipped up by a light sea-breeze, Burton now had two of the board riders, astride their plastic planks, on either side of her tail where the flukes narrowed in to join the body.

"Christ," he muttered to himself. "If she does do her block and let fly we'll all be killed."

The surfers were oblivious to the danger, completely absorbed in what they were doing at Burton's bidding.

It took them fifteen minutes to wrestle the chunky rope twice around Nika's tail and bring the two eyes together. Burton then passed the cable through the eyes and began to haul back towards the Star.

"Thanks fellas. You'd better keep pretty well back from her. She might decide to throw herself around a bit."

They moved back.

BLUE WHALE

Nika just wallowed. She was crying out all the time now. Long, deep intense sounds no human could hear.

When Burton reached the ship Alison left the wheel, took a line attached to the cable and made it fast onto the Star's stern bollard. While Burton climbed aboard she went back to the wheelhouse. They didn't speak.

He hauled the cable aboard and struggled to make it fast so that it now snaked out in long loop, from the winch, to the whale, through the eyes in the rope and back to the ship.

He checked the fastening. "Right–o, Al. Give it a try."

Alison eased the Star forward till the cable tightened like a violin string and then revved the engines to full ahead.

The whale didn't budge.

Nika cried out in pain as the cable tore at her muscles and the rope burned the skin around her tail. She was puzzled and had no inclination to help the ship, if it was trying to pull her out to sea. She was resolved to stay stuck in the sand. The pain of the ship heaving at her was no worse than the oil and the agonising burden of her immense body pressing down on her lungs and belly.

Alison eased off.

Under the idling growl of the Gascoyne Star's engines Nika heard the faint, far off sound of a whale. She listened and wished that the ship would stop the noise that was overpowering the soft call.

Nika focused in the direction of the call and whaled her hardest, long and strong. And back through the water, clearly now, came the sound of Musco. She listened again and she was sure. It was Musco. And he was sure it was Nika.

He was calling to her and she could hear the booming surge of joy in his call. She called back. There was reason again for Nika to live.

Burton noticed that the whale was trying to move. For the first time there was a twitch in the flukes and she was trying to squirm in the sand.

"By Christ, Al. She wants to come out," he said. "Give it another go now. If she's going to help, it just might do the trick."

The Gascoyne Star roared again and churned up sand and debris as her screws turned and the cable strained. The whale threw her head to the left, then to the right.

Alison pushed the throttle as far as it would go and there was a jerk forward.

"She's moved," Alison screamed.

"It wasn't the cable giving?" Burton asked, as he picked himself up from the wheelhouse deck. "Here. Give us a go."

"No Alan. I'm going to do it."

The crowd on the beach—who a short while ago would have been just as happy to have carved their initials on the whale's side had they been able to reach her—began to cheer. Like a football crowd, they liked to support an underdog and it looked as though the whale might just win.

The crowd and Alison and Burton were concentrating on the struggle to free the whale, boosted by that small jerk towards success. Nobody noticed the waft of white spout thirty feet into the air and disappear. Only a little way out to sea, it was far beyond their attention.

The whale wriggled in the sand again and the Gascoyne Star roared. There was another jerk and the crowd cheered.

Then they were silent.

Burton almost lost his footing and slipped down the wheelhouse ladder when he saw it and Alison just gaped. So did the crowd on the beach who gaped and pointed.

Alongside the Gascoyne Star a great spout shot skywards as Musco breached almost lazily. Here, on board the ship, close to a beach, close to buildings and other people, there was an immediate perspective. And Musco's one hundred and twenty foot length was exposed in the clear shallow water. He was gargantuan and at this range his size took Burton's breath away.

Alison stole a glance and she remembered the day in the zodiac when she saw the long pale scar which streaked Musco's back.

"It's the same one," she said.

"You're right," said Burton still agape and breathless, unable to take his eyes off Musco.

Musco had stopped moving forward almost the moment he breached and blew and now, with only his flippers moving he seemed to be sizing up the situation.

Under the water Musco and Nika were locked in a telepathic embrace. He was far bigger than she and it was impossible for him to reach her without beaching himself. It was agonising, after all they had lost, to rejoin this much without being able to touch each other. He comforted her with thoughts of sympathy and love and reassurance.

Alison fired the Gascoyne Star again and Musco saw what was happening.

Nika had all but forgotten the pain and suffocating effects of the oil, the excruciation of the tug between her and the Gascoyne Star. With Musco here she would be safe. She had no doubt. They would swim on, together again.

While the ship shuddered and the cable twanged taut, Musco wheeled about and began to edge backwards slowly towards Nika.

Alison, staggered by what seemed about to happen, eased off on the throttle to watch. But not so much that she lost the tension on the cable.

As he got closer to Nika, Musco began to make great horizontal sweeps with his tail, which he held as close as he could to the sandy bottom. The motion of his tail drove him back out towards the ship. He edged in again towards Nika. And again he made sweeps with his tail, stirring up a maelstrom of water and debris.

"He's digging her a channel, for Christ sake. He's digging her a channel." Alison shook her head in disbelief.

Burton was now down on the stern deck watching, slack jawed at what he saw. On the beach people were dashing into the water and cheering and leaping in support of the great whales.

Musco came in again, carefully following the channel that he'd dug towards Nika. And there was more threshing and more swirling water and sand. And he was a little closer to his mate.

All the time he was digging and swimming he was locked into Nika's mind, moaning love songs and calls of encouragement to her.

Alison saw how close they were and thought the sand might give now. She waited for Musco to fall back under the force of his tail strokes and then revved the Star again.

This time there was no jerk, but a steady almost unnoticeable giving of the great beached body.

Musco moved in backwards again, quicker this time and he almost reached Nika's tail. She started to slide.

"Go Alison, go," Burton screamed.

Musco went in again and this time he jammed his flukes under her tail and writhed for all he was worth, like a monstrous minnow just out of the water. Nika moved a little more. And Musco dug a little more. Alison kept on full throttle at the wheel of the Gascoyne Star.

Nika took up a gentle side to side motion again, as if to help too, but Musco stopped her. He did not want her to do anything to make her suffer more.

"She's coming. She's moving," Alison shrieked.

Nika was, slowly sliding out along the channel Musco had dug for her. She moved, tail-first, following Musco.

The crowd went mad, car horns honked, people screamed with delight, pranced on the sand and danced into the water. When the boat reached deep water Burton let go the cable. It whipped out across the surface and quickly slipped the eyes of the rope hawser.

Musco was nuzzling and stroking Nika. He rubbed himself along her entire length and realised that the hawser was still tightly wrapped around her tail. He flicked at it with a fluke and sent one end of the rope whipping up out of the water and splashing down on the other side. He swam along the full length of Nika, rubbing her gently with his body and stroking her with his flipper. He stopped to nuzzle her around her great grinning jaw and swam down her length on the other side.

He flicked the other end of the hawser.

Then Nika began to wriggle and the rope was free, sinking to the bottom.

Physically, Nika was almost on the brink between life and death but with Musco fussing and fretting about her she had regained her spirit. With Musco and a purpose in life again her body would make its repairs. She was very sore, and she was exhausted but she wanted to swim with Musco to the Chagos Archipelago.

They turned for the open sea but before he dived Musco swam up alongside the Gascoyne Star. His massive head rose up out of the water and threw a shadow across the stern of the boat. Standing in the shadow, Alison and Burton stared into the flat blue-grey eye which gazed at them.

They saw love. And they saw inside the whale. For a moment, together, that barrier between people and whales was gone. Alison and Burton were inside the whale's mind; he in theirs. And they knew whaleness.

Then Musco and Nika were gone. Two eddies swirled where their tails slipped beneath the chop of the waves.